DATE DUE

MAR 2 2 2001		
MAR 1 2003		
MAR 2 1 2003		
NOV 0 4 2003		

398.9
Des

Desmond, Sean
Touch of the Irish

Maysville R-I High School

TOUCH
of the IRISH

Other books on the Irish from Random House Value Publishing, Inc.:

THE IRISH SPIRIT

IRISH WONDERS

A TREASURY OF IRISH MYTH, LEGEND, AND FOLKLORE

IRISH BLESSINGS

TOUCH
of the IRISH

Sean Desmond

Illustrated with engravings by Robert Gibbings

GRAMERCY BOOKS
New York

This 1999 edition is published by Gramercy Books™, an imprint of Random House Value Publishing, Inc., 201 East 50th Street, New York, NY 10022, by arrangement with Michael O'Mara Books Limited, Great Britain.

Gramercy Books™ and design are trademarks of Random House Value Publishing, Inc.

Printed in the United States of America

Random House
New York • Toronto • London • Sydney • Auckland
http://www.randomhouse.com/

A CIP catalog record for this book is available from the Library of Congress

ISBN 0-517-20653-6

8 7 6 5 4 3 2 1

CONTENTS

♣

INTRODUCTION

♣

... the great Gaels of Ireland
Are the men that God made mad,
For all their wars are merry,
And all their songs are sad.

G K Chesterton was not entirely right when he wrote
those words in 'The Ballad of the White Horse'. In the
land of the jig, it would hardly be possible for literally
every song to be sad. For all the mournful pipers in
the mountains, there are at least as many merry
fiddlers at the crossroads. But, beneath his
lighthearted hyperbole, the great Catholic Englishman
was expressing a more profound and irrefutable
truth. The essence of all Irish wisdom is a constant
awareness of the potential heartbreak that lies in wait
on the edge of all happiness; and the essence of all
Irish wit is a capacity to smile in the face of adversity.

For those who like that sort of thing, there has
always been plenty to suffer in Ireland. The island lies
out on the farthest edge of Europe, screening the
ungrateful continent from the worst of the Atlantic's
winds and rains. To the north and west and south of
her there is nothing but ocean as far as the horizon;
and beyond the horizon there is nothing but
Greenland, America and Africa. And to the east, a
bit too close for comfort, there is the lowering land
mass that gave her only one gift, a religion, and took
in return, for ever after, her multitude of saints
and soldiers.

Assailed from the west by the worst of weather
and from the east, despite her inhospitable solitude,
by generations of Nordic raiders and invaders, Ireland
has had little experience of prosperity or peace. But
her people have made the most of their misfortune.
They have emerged grinning from their long painful
history with a mythology as developed as the Greeks',
a faith firmer than Rome's, a benign fatalism worthy
of the Lord Buddha himself and a sense of urgency
so under-developed that it makes even a Mexican
look manic.

The unique history has engendered a unique
humour. Irish wit is gentle. Even the sharpest and
deepest jibes are delivered with such deceptive self-
effacing charm that the uninitiated often join in the
laughter without realizing that they are the butt of it.

At the heart of the typical Irish joke there is a
similarly deceptive humility, an intentional
misunderstanding, which uncomprehending
comedians all over the world have broadened into a
crude stupidity. In night clubs and variety theatres
from Adelaide to Amsterdam, comedians from every
country but Ireland describe a dope ring as six
Irishmen in a circle and tell about the Irish jellyfish
that set, the Irish parachute that opens on impact and
the Irish attempt on Mount Everest that failed when
the climbers ran out of scaffolding.

But the mistakes and misunderstandings in the
true Irish joke are at the same time more whimsical
and more significant. For example, there was a story
going around Dublin a couple of years ago about a

priest whose car ran out of petrol a few yards from his house. Knowing that his lawn-mower probably contained enough fuel to get him to the nearest gas station, he went back to fetch it and, for want of any other receptacle, used the old chamberpot from under his bed. Some minutes later, a farmer came along with his horse drawn cart, halted it beside the car and stared at the priest pouring the contents of a chamberpot into the petrol tank. 'Begob, father,' said he, 'I wish I had your faith.'

And then there was the equally typical story about the schoolmaster who always drank in the bar eight miles from his home because the beer there was ten pence a pint cheaper than in the one close by. When someone pointed out that the bus fare there and back was ninety pence, he simply said, 'So what? I go on drinking till I make a profit.'

The sad thing is that the books of Irish wit and wisdom that have been coming out all too often recently have done nothing more than regurgitate the same old comedians' patter, and their more weighty witticisms have only been quotations from the works of the greatest Irish playwrights. But the words which Sheridan, Wilde and Shaw put into the mouths of London society have no more to do with Ireland than the daft jokes. The Ireland of these books is the Ireland of the Saint Patrick's Day Parade on Fifth Avenue or wherever, the Ireland that never existed anywhere outside the imagination of Walt Disney.

That is why I had to compile this book for you. The Ireland here is the Ireland of Caitlin ni Uallachain and mists and widows. This is the Ireland that has existed for as long as the sea has let her. All the anecdotes here have at least some claim to authenticity. They come from newspapers, law-reports, memoirs or letters. The words of the great wits are not the written words for which they were paid but the words that they spoke in conversation in the greatest of all Irish art-forms, 'the repartee'. And the proverbs and the curses and the cures are as old and as tried and as true as granite.

This is a book too rich to be taken from start to finish at one sitting. The way to read it is to skip about in it, sampling here and there and coming back to favourites like a child at a wedding feast. In the welcoming words of what is said to be the oldest fragment of verse in the English language...

> I am of Ireland
> and of the holy land
> of Ireland.
> Good Sir, I pray thee,
> For of Saint Charity,
> Come and dance with me
> In Ireland.

Sean Desmond

THE POLITICS

♣

There were several great Irish orators and wits in the British Parliament at the end of the eighteenth century, including Edmund Burke and the playwright Richard Brinsley Sheridan, but the one who most consistently provided the House with harmless pleasure was Sir Boyle Roche, the member for Cork. The following are just a few selections from his many immortal speeches.

The cup of old Ireland's miseries has been overflowing for centuries and it is not yet full.

The country is overrun by absentee landlords.

With trial by jury I have lived and by God with trial by jury I shall die.

Half the lies our opponents tell about us are not true.

It would be better, Mr. Speaker, to give up not only a part but, if necessary, even

the whole of our constitution in order to preserve
the remainder.

I concluded from the very beginning that this
would be the end of the matter and I see now that
I was right, for it is not half over yet.

All along the untrodden paths of the future I can
see the footprints of an unseen hand.

Once they abolish hanging in this country they will
have to hang twice as many.

The profligacy of the age is such that we see little children who can neither walk nor talk running around the streets cursing their maker.

Anyone who wishes to diminish the brotherly affection of our two sister countries is an enemy of both nations.

Sir Boyle was not always unintentionally funny, particularly when he was angry. Once, when he was making a speech to the House of Commons, the opposition tried to drown him out with coughing. Eventually Sir Boyle, who was as ready for a drink or a duel as any man in Ireland, pulled a fistful of pistol-bullets from his pocket and waved them at his tormentors. 'These are infallible cures for a cough,' said he, 'and I will be happy to administer them if any of the gentlemen opposite would care to try them.'

At the end of the following century, Colonel Sanderson MP attempted to keep up Sir Boyle's great tradition with: 'I was born Irish and have been so ever since.'

The tradition continues. Not so long ago an Ulster MP decried the treatment of political prisoners thus, 'We have to go back centuries for an equivalent to such treatment, and even then we don't find it.'

Another great Irish wit in the House of Commons at the end of the eighteenth century was John Philpot

Curran, although his sharp tongue was more often deadly in law courts and drawing rooms than in Parliament. When he once said that, like most Irishmen, he could not speak in public for more than a quarter of an hour without moistening his lips, Sir Thomas Turton replied, 'I have the advantage of you there, Curran. I spoke in the House the other night for five hours on the Nabob of Oude and never felt in the least bit thirsty.'

'That is very remarkable indeed,' said Curran, 'For everyone else agrees that it was the driest speech of the session.'

The greatest of all the Irish wits in the English House of Commons was without doubt Richard Brinsley Sheridan. He was at his best demolishing propositions with long, mocking and consistently funny speeches, all of which were too long to quote here, but there were a few 'one-liners'. An ardent admirer of George Washington, he destroyed Mr Dundas's sneering speech in support of Lord North's war in America with a simple, 'The Right Honourable gentleman is indebted to his memory for his jests and to his imagination for his facts.'

However, the greatest of the late eighteenth century Irish orators was Edmund Burke. Burke was another supporter of the American colonists. After the United States had achieved independence in the Treaty of Paris, he made a profoundly prophetic speech in favour of 'conciliation ', in which he said, 'There is

America, which at this day serves for little more than to amuse you with stories of savage men and uncouth manners, yet shall, before you taste of death, show itself equal to the whole of that commerce which now attracts the envy of the world.'

Burke had as much of an instinct for aphorisms as Roche had for unintentional humour:

People will not look forward to posterity who never look backward to their ancestors.

There never was a bad man that had ability for good service.

Kings will be tyrants from policy when subjects are rebels from principle.

Early and provident fear is the mother of safety.

Great men will never do great mischief but for some great end.

A candidate in Kerry is said to have dismissed a parliamentary report as 'an entirely garbled account of what never took place '.

The great political difference between England and Ireland, it is said, is that in England you can say what you like so long as you do

the right thing and in Ireland you can do what you like so long as you say the right thing.

Charles Stewart Parnell once wound up a parliamentary committee with the words, 'Gentlemen, we are unanimous that we cannot agree.'

Political correctness came early to Ireland. In the 1890s, when the campaign for women's suffrage was

in its infancy, a Wexford shopkeeper put the following notice above his door: 'Women, without distinction of sex, will be equally served.'

A Member of Parliament for Limerick in the nineteenth century is reported as having contemplated his third election campaign with complete confidence. 'The poor have always voted for me,' he said. 'And there are more poor today than ever.'

Irishness can be contagious. During the 1916 rebellion the British Parliament passed an act providing for the building of a new, larger prison in Dublin. Part I of the act ruled that the materials from the old buildings were to be used in the construction of the new ones. Part II provided that prisoners should be kept in the old buildings until the new ones were finished.

When asked to define the English Ascendancy, playwright Brendan Behan replied, 'A Protestant on a horse.'

THE IRISH IN COURT

♣

In a Limerick court at the end of the last century, a judge dismissed the accused with the words, 'You go from this court with no stain on your character other than that you have been acquitted by an Irish jury.'

A judge once asked the occupant of a Dublin tenement how he could possibly claim that he only threw his wife out of a second-storey window out of forgetfulness.

'Well, you see, your lordship,' said he, 'we only moved in a week ago and we used to live on the ground floor.'

At Dublin Assizes, a man convicted of bigamy pleaded with the judge before sentence. 'My lord, I was only trying to get a good one.'

The famous and popular Irish judge Lord Morris once interrupted in the examination of a doctor who had been accused of administering a fatal dose of dope to a racehorse. 'Surely, doctor, a dozen grains of a poison as strong as that would be enough to kill the devil himself?'

Eager to get the better of the great man, the doctor answered with a sneer, 'I don't know, my lord. I've never prescribed for the devil.'

'Ah, no,' said Lord Morris, 'nor you have, more's the pity. I was forgetting the old boy is still alive.'

Another great hero of the Irish bar was John Philpot Curran, who practised at the end of the eighteenth century. When a pompous prosecutor told him that he would put him in his pocket if he continued to provoke him, Curran replied, 'If you do that, you will have more law in your pocket than you ever had in your head.'

Mr Justice Fitzgibbon, who later became Lord Chancellor, once dismissed Curran's argument with, 'If that be the law, Mr Curran, I may burn my law books.' To which Curran retorted, 'You had better read them first, my lord.'

When he sat as Lord Chancellor, Fitzgibbon often took his favourite dog with him into court. On one occasion, when Curran was addressing him, Fitzgibbon looked down at his dog and began to pat and stroke him. At this, Curran fell silent.

'Why do you not proceed, Mr Curran?' said Fitzgibbon.

Curran bowed. 'I thought your lordships were in consultation.'

An exasperated judge once told Curran that if he said another word he would commit him.

'If your lordship does that,' said Curran, 'we shall both of us have the consolation of knowing that I am not the worst thing your lordship has committed.'

When one of his more idiotic colleagues suggested that only men who owned landed estates and were therefore independent should be admitted to the bar, Curran answered, 'May I ask, sir, how many acres make a wiseacre?'

Addressing a court on a difficult matter of ecclesiastical law, Curran noticed a very tall, thin barrister behind him, who he knew had been studying for Holy Orders before changing to read for the bar. 'I would like to refer your lordship to a high authority behind me,' said he. 'He was himself intended for the church, although in my opinion he was fitter for the steeple.'

Dining at the Middle Temple one day, the famous Irish 'hanging judge' Lord Norbury rejected the pheasant on the grounds that it had not been hung. 'Ah now,' said Curran from the other end of the table, 'your lordship has only to try it and it will be hung for sure.'

Norbury was a notorious duellist. Curran said of him that he had 'shot himself up to the bench', and even after he had reached it he would challenge any barrister who presumed to dispute his rulings with 'Name any hour before my court opens tomorrow, sir.' He was always ready to show his contempt for anyone who avoided the field of honour, even when it was a demonstrably brave man like Daniel O'Connell.

The remorseful Nationalist leader had sworn never to fight again after killing his Unionist opponent in his first duel, but within months he had accepted a challenge from Sir Robert Peel, then Chief Secretary for Ireland, whom he had insulted in a debate. However, while on his way to meet Peel in France, where duelling was still legal, O'Connell stopped off in London, where he was detained by a magistrate who somehow discovered his purpose, ordered his arrest and bound him over to keep the peace.

Back in Dublin, O'Connell continued his career at the bar, and when he next appeared before Norbury, there was a moment when it seemed that the judge had failed to understand his argument.

'Pardon me, my lord,' said O'Connell. 'I am afraid your lordship does not apprehend me.'

'Pardon me also,' said Norbury. 'There is no man more easily apprehended than Mr O'Connell... whenever he wishes to be apprehended.'

At the end of the last century an English Resident Magistrate in Kerry asked a farmer who had chosen to conduct his own defence whether he pleaded guilty or not guilty to the charge of assault.

'Oh indeed I am innocent, your honour,' said the

farmer. 'Sure if I was guilty I'd have found me a lawyer.'

Another man charged with assault, this time in Carlow, informed the court that he would not know whether to plead guilty or not guilty until he had heard the evidence.

In a similar case in Cork, the judge warned the accused that it was dangerous to represent himself on so serious a charge.

'Ah, thank you, your honour,' said the accused. 'That's very kind, but I assure you there's no need to worry. I may have no counsel, but I have several good friends on the jury.'

In another case in Cork a judge asked the accused if there was anyone in court who could vouch for his good character.

'Yes, my lord,' said the rogue pointing at the Chief Constable, 'that gentleman there.'

The city's senior police officer rose with obvious embarrassment and told the court that he had never seen or heard of the man before in his life.

'There you are, my lord,' said the accused. 'What more can you ask? I've lived in this city some twenty years and I'm completely unknown to the police.'

Pressed by his busy schedule, a Protestant circuit judge once attempted to hold a court on Good Friday.

'If you go ahead with this,' said the leader of the many objecting barristers, 'your lordship will be the first judge to have sat on this day since Pontius Pilate.'

Horrified by the huge pile of documentary evidence which a witness had suddenly produced, a judge asked if he could give the court the gist of its contents.

'Well, not really, your honour,' said the witness frowning. 'It's all gist.'

In challenging an Irish doctor's evidence, a barrister asked him if doctors did not sometimes make mistakes.

'Yes,' said the doctor, 'and so do lawyers.'

'But doctors' mistakes are buried six foot under,' said the barrister.

'So are lawyers',' said the doctor. 'The only difference is that the lawyers' mistakes swing first.'

Passing judgment in a maintenance case, a judge awarded the abandoned wife £1 a week. 'Ah, that's very kind of your honour,' said the defendant. 'I'll try to find a few pennies for her myself.'

At the beginning of the last century a famous judge, Chief Baron O'Grady, was trying a highwayman at Kilkenny Assizes. On the evidence the man was clearly guilty, but to the judge's amazement the jury found him not guilty. 'Tell the jailor not to let him loose till I have half an hour's start on him,' said the judge. 'I'd rather not meet him on the road.'
On another occasion, also at Kilkenny Assizes,

O'Grady made fun of a precocious young barrister. While the young man was addressing the jury, a donkey on the green outside began to bray. 'Wait a minute please, Mr Bush,' said the judge. 'I can't hear two at a time.' But young Charles Kendal Bush, later Chief Justice of the King's Bench, was more than a match for O'Grady. When the judge was summing up, the donkey brayed again. 'Would your lordship please speak a little louder,' said Bush. 'There is such an echo in the court.'

In later life, the poet Michael Joseph Barry became a police magistrate in Dublin. During the Fenian rising of 1867, an American was brought before him on a charge of sedition. On asking the arresting officer for his basis for the charge, Barry was informed that the accused was wearing 'a Republican hat'.

'I am not sure that I understand you,' said Barry. 'I presume that a Republican hat is a hat with no crown.'

Prosecuting counsel told a man in County Clare that he could produce two witnesses who had seen him steal the disputed spade.

'That's nothing,' said the accused. 'I can find a dozen who didn't.'

'This court can have no sympathy for a man who beats his wife,' said a resident magistrate.

'That's all right, your honour,' said the accused. 'Any man who can beat his wife doesn't need sympathy.'

A man was being tried at Cork Quarter Sessions for stealing ducks from a farm. The farmer claimed that he could recognize his ducks anywhere because he had bred them with their own distinctive markings.

'But I have ducks like that on my own farm,' said defending counsel after the farmer had described them.

'Sure I wouldn't be a bit surprised,' said the farmer. 'It's not the first time I've been robbed.'

A Donegal jury brought in the following verdict: 'We find that the man who stole the mare is not guilty.'

Protesting vehemently that he was not incapacitated by drink, the accused told a Dublin court, 'I was sober enough to know I was drunk.'

In a murder trial at Galway Assizes, prosecuting counsel was pressing a witness for the defence, who claimed that the pistol found in his possession had not been acquired for any felonious intent. 'Come now,' said the prosecutor. 'On your solemn oath, what did you get the weapon for?'

'On my solemn oath,' said the dignified witness, 'I got it for three shillings in Richardson's pawn-office.'

In the early part of this century the proceedings in Galway courts were often disrupted by the effects of intoxicating liquors. One Friday afternoon, after several persons in the public gallery had questioned the judge's legitimacy, his lordship ordered the clerk to clear the court. The clerk rose unsteadily and announced, 'All you bastards that aren't lawyers get out.'

On entering the witness box, a Dubliner declined to answer any questions for fear that his slurred speech might reveal his condition.

'This is contempt of court,' said the judge.

'I know it is, my lord,' said the witness, 'but I was endeavouring to conceal it.'

 After listening to the schoolmaster, the priest, the publican and most of the other respectable residents of the

village, all of whom had come to attest to the good character of the accused, Mr Justice Lawson turned to the twelve men on his left. 'Gentlemen of the jury, I think the only conclusion you can arrive at is this: the pig was stolen by the most amiable man in County Mayo.'

'It is a sad thing,' said the Recorder of Dublin, 'to see a young man like you lose character, prospects and everything for the sake of seven pence.'

'That's not my fault,' said the young felon whom he was about to sentence.

'Why's that?' said the judge.

'Sure I wouldn't have robbed the till at all if I'd known there was no more than that in it.'

A pedantic and impatient judge once interrupted the barrister who was defending a simple farm hand. 'Mr O'Connor, has your client never heard of the maxim *sic utere tuo alienum non laudas*?'

'Indeed, my lord,' said counsel earnestly, 'in the Mushera Mountains where Paddy lives they speak of little else.'

The alcoholic madame of a popular Dublin brothel at the turn of the century was prepared to take yet another sentence with her usual studied dignity, but she lost her temper when the magistrate presumed to call her a disgrace to the city. 'If it wasn't for me and the likes of me,' she snapped, 'there'd be little use for police and the likes of you. It's people like me that puts food in your mouths and all we gets is jailing and impudence.'

Seeing a circuit judge quenching his thirst with coffee on a hot day, a young barrister asked if he had ever tried a long cool gin and tonic.

'I have not,' said the judge, 'but I have tried several fellows who have.'

A resident magistrate warned the accused that a hundred years ago horse-stealing was a hanging offence.

'Exactly, your honour,' said the accused. 'And a hundred years from now, who knows, it might not be an offence at all.'

English judges were seldom comfortable in Irish courts. One who chose to admonish the accused for having hit a man much smaller than himself received the answer, 'Well what would your lordship have done if he'd called you an Irish slob?'

'But I'm not an Irishman,' said the judge.

'Well suppose he called you a Welsh slob then?'

'I'm not a Welshman.'

'Well then,' said the exasperated accused, 'suppose he called you whatever kind of slob you are?'

English barristers fared little better. A Victorian QC asked a difficult witness in Cork, 'Are you not aware that you are commanded by the Holy Book not to bear false witness against your neighbour?'

'Indeed I am, your worship sir,' said the witness. 'But sure I'm not bearing false witness against him, I'm bearing it for him.'

For hundreds of years it was said in Ireland that one of Saint Patrick's responsibilities in Paradise was to take care of the fence between Heaven and Hell. After failing many times to get the devil to keep his side in good repair, the saint threatened to sue if the work was not done.

'Will you now,' said the devil. 'And where on your side will you find a lawyer?'

A Kerry coroner once brought in the following verdict on a drowned drunk. 'The deceased was killed by an act of God under very suspicious circumstances.'

On what promised to be the last day of a long trial, a circuit judge in Limerick noticed that he now had only eleven jurors. When he enquired as to the whereabouts of the twelfth man, the foreman answered, 'He is a huntsman and has gone to the meet, your honour. But 'tis no matter. He has written down his verdict and left it with me.'

THE IRISH AT WAR

♣

It has long been said that the Irish are only at peace when they are fighting.

Perhaps the most famous mercenaries in history were the Irish 'Wilde Geese', who fought for most of the European monarchies, particularly France. When an exasperated King Louis XIV told one of their senior commanders that his rowdy and exuberant Irish soldiers gave him more trouble than the whole of the rest of the French army put together, Count Mahoney

replied, 'Indeed, your
Majesty. Your enemies
say that as well.'

The famous definition
of the Cork Militia was
that it was as useless in
war as it was dangerous
in peace.

An aristocratic lady who
lived near the city of Cork in the middle of the last
century sent a servant to the barracks of the Cork
Militia with a note 'requesting the pleasure of Captain
Bourke's company to dinner'. He was met by a
sergeant, who opened the note, and when the servant
returned with an answer his mistress was surprised to
read as follows:

'Privates Hennessy and O'Brien are unable to
accept, owing to their being on duty; but the
remainder of Captain Bourke's company will have
much pleasure in accepting your ladyship's hospitality.'

In the aftermath of the Battle of Minden an agonized
Irish voice was heard calling out to the loudest of the
many moaning wounded on the field, 'Will you shut
that din there. You'd think you were the only man
here that was killed.'

Returning from the Seven-Years' War, an Irish soldier
went into a London tavern and showed off the hole

made by a musket
ball in the top of
his tall mitre cap.
'Just think of it,'
said he, 'if I'd been
wearing a low
bonnet, I'd have
been killed for sure.'

The eighteenth-century British admiral Lord Howe
recorded that he had heard an Irish sailor intoning
the following prayer before the night watch: 'Lord, I
never murdered any man and no man murdered me,
so God bless all mankind.'

During the 1798 rebellion, the inimitable Sir Boyle
Roche MP wrote a dramatic letter to a friend in
London. The following are a few extracts.

'While I write this letter, I hold a sword in one
hand and a pistol in the other... I should have
answered your letter a fortnight ago, but I only
received it this morning. Indeed hardly a mail arrives
safely without being robbed... Last Thursday an
alarm was given that a gang of rebels were advancing
hither under the French flag, but they had no colours
nor any drums except bagpipes. Immediately every
man in the place, including women and boys, ran out
to meet them... Fortunately the rebels had no weapons
but guns, cutlasses and pikes, and as we had plenty of
muskets and ammunition, we put them all to the
sword. Not a soul of them escaped, except some that

were drowned in an adjacent bog, and in a very short time there was nothing to be heard but silence.'

Soon afterwards Sir Boyle submitted the following brilliant plan for keeping smugglers out of the River Shannon. 'I would anchor a frigate off each bank of the river with strict orders not to stir, and so by cruising up and down I would put a stop to their trade.'

During the First World War, the following exchange was heard in the darkness of 'No-Man's Land' as an Irish night patrol returned to its trenches:
    'Will you come on, Jack?'
    'I can't.'
    'Why not?'
    'I've taken a prisoner.'
    'Well, bring him with you.'
    'I can't.'
    'Why not?'
    'He won't come.'
    'So come without him.'
    'I can't.'
    'Why not?'
    'He won't let me.'

Despite Ireland's neutrality in the Second World War, a large number of Irish volunteers fought gallantly for the allies. During a particularly ill-fated air

raid over Germany, when flak and night-fighters were taking a terrible toll among allied bombers, an Irish gunner's voice was heard muttering on a Lancaster's intercom. 'Mary, Jesus and Joseph, this is the worst bloody war ever. Thank God De Valera kept us out of it.'

When an Irish soldier asked his platoon commander for compassionate leave to visit his wife, who was about to give birth, the officer replied that he could not do so since he had received a letter from the soldier's wife specifically requesting that he should on no account be allowed to go home.

'By God, sir,' said the soldier, 'I respect that entirely. You're as good a liar as I am any day. Sure I was never married.'

The age-old motto of the Irish soldier: help a woman and hit a man.

It is the pup's mother that teaches him to fight.

Defending himself on a charge of striking a fellow soldier, an Irish recruit pleaded, 'I thought there was no harm in it. Sure all I had in my hand was my fist.'

One of the greatest of Ireland's many great soldiers, the Duke of Wellington, said that 'nothing except a battle lost can be half so melancholy as a battle won'.

Oscar Wilde took a slightly more cynical view. 'As long as war is regarded as wicked, it will always have its fascination. When it is looked upon as vulgar, it will cease to be popular.'

On a visit to London during the Second World War, Bishop James Pike was walking along Whitehall with a young friend who was then serving as a captain in the Irish Guards. As they walked between the huge buildings that house the great offices of state, the bishop turned to his companion and asked, 'On which side is the War Office, do you know?'

'Good God,' said the captain, 'Ours I hope.'

Before 1916 the epitaph for all Irish soldiers was: 'We fought every nation's battles and the only ones that we lost were our own.'

THE FAITH AND THE CLERGY

♣

A Protestant rector spent a year in his new Ulster parish without ever exchanging a single word with the Catholic priest with whom he shared it. At last he screwed up the courage to confront the priest in the street and suggest that they ought to be on speaking terms. 'After all,' he said, 'we are both in the same business.'

'That's right,' said the priest, 'indeed we are. You're doing it your way, and I'm doing it His.'

A young woman confessed the sin of vanity to the famous Father James Healy, parish priest of Bray.

'And how does this vanity display itself?' asked the father.

'Every morning, Father, I stand in front of the glass and I admire what I see.'

'Oh, don't worry about that,' said Father Healy. 'That's not a sin. That's just a mistake.'

The Protestant Vicar of Bray once said to Father Healy that he had been sixty years in the world and had not yet discovered the difference between a good Catholic and a good Protestant.

'Is that right?' said Father Healy. 'Well, you won't be sixty seconds in the next world before you do.'

Contemplating death, Father Healy admitted, 'I would prefer Heaven for climate but Hell for society: all my best friends are Protestants.'

Soon after his appointment, Archbishop Patrick Ryan of Baltimore went to a reception where a jovial politician said to him, 'Now where in hell have I seen you before?'

'I don't know,' said the Archbishop. 'Where in hell do you come from?'

While canvassing for a general election, a Unionist candidate entered one of the many houses in the South Belfast constituency in which the husband and wife were of different religions. Above the

fireplace in the living room there was a portrait of the Pope, and on the opposite wall a picture of the Protestant hero King William III on his white horse.

The candidate looked at the pictures with amusement. 'It is good to see such harmony,' he said.

'Oh there's no trouble between us,' said the woman of the house, 'except on the 12th of July of course.'

'What happens then?'

'Well he goes on the march and gets drunk with the rest of his Orangemen and then he comes home and pulls down the picture of His Holiness and stamps all over it and then goes up and passes out on the bed ... But it's no matter. He always pays for it without a murmur.'

'He does?'

'Oh yes. Next day I get up before him and take the picture of King Billy into town and pawn it. And then with the money I buy a new picture of His Holiness. And then when himself gets up I give him the pawn ticket and he goes down the town and redeems King Billy.'

A nineteenth-century Dublin bishop wrote the following little verse shortly before his death:

Tell my priests when I am gone
O'er me to shed no tears.
For I shall be no deader then
Than they have been for years.

Travelling by train in an enclosed compartment, Cardinal Richard Cushing asked the frail young Jesuit who accompanied him whether he would mind if he smoked a cigar.

'Oh, no, Your Eminence,' said his companion. 'Not if you don't mind my being sick.'

A Belfast Catholic once asked a Church of Ireland minister, 'Where was your religion before King Henry VIII and Martin Luther?'

'Did you wash your face this morning?' said the rector.

'I did.'

'And where was your face before you washed it?'

Another Belfast Catholic, this time a builder, described the best day's work he had ever done as 'pulling down a Protestant church and getting paid for it'.

Congratulating a visiting bishop on his moving sermon, a woman from Wexford told him it was 'like water to a drowning man'.

When the Protestant parish council of Ballymoney
was building a new school, one of the members of the
council found an appropriate quotation from the poet
Alexander Pope to have carved above the door.
Although not entirely sure what it meant, the other
councillors agreed, and when the building was
finished the following appeared in a plaque beneath
the arch of the entrance:

> A little learning is a dangerous thing:
> drink deep, or taste not the Pierian spring
> *A Pope*

To the astonishment of the council and the two new
teachers, the school was completely unattended
throughout its first week of opening. However, after

making enquiries in church that Sunday they discovered that there was not a Protestant parent in the village who was prepared to send a child to a school that had the words of a Roman pontiff above the door.

After telling a Belfast congregation that the subject of his sermon was to be lying, a visiting preacher asked how many of those present had read the seventeenth chapter of the Gospel according to St Mark. At least two thirds of them raised a hand.

'Good,' said he, 'I have chosen the right subject for this congregation. There are only sixteen chapters in St Mark's gospel.'

Maurice Healy, the famous Irish KC and author, once asked the Belfast barrister John Bartley to explain the difference between a Calvinist and an ordinary Presbyterian.

'Well,' said Bartley, 'a Calvinist believes that all Catholics will be damned because they're predestined to be damned, and an ordinary Presbyterian believes that they will be damned on their merits.'

Bidding farewell to a parish priest who was leaving to be installed as a bishop, a parishioner told him, 'We owe a lot to you, Father. We knew nothing about sin till you came to the parish.'

'Your Lordship has taken great trouble and we are all very grateful to you,' said the parishioner thanking the bishop for taking services on a Sunday when the parish priest was sick. 'A worse man would have done, but we couldn't find one.'

A Protestant clergyman in Newry recounted a meeting with two Catholic children in the street.

'Good morning, Father,' said one of them, respectfully stepping out of his way.

The reverend gentleman returned the greeting, but as he walked on he heard the other child remonstrating with his fellow.

'What did you call him father for? He's no father. He's got five children.'

LOVE AND MARRIAGE

♣

In Ireland the village priest is the man to whom everyone turns with every problem except one. If you cannot find a wife or a husband, you go instead to a matchmaker, for it has long been said that a priest's match always leads to an unhappy marriage.

 All women have the same strategy. They begin by blocking a man's advances and end by blocking his retreat.

A man can only be a man when his woman is a woman.

No Irishman ever fell in love at first sight in broad daylight.

At one of his many parties, Richard Brinsley Sheridan once said to a young lady, 'Won't you come into the garden? I should like my roses to see you.'

Courtship in Ireland is said to be that period during which a girl decides whether or not she can do any better.

It is said that proud Irishmen used to propose marriage by asking, 'How would you like to be buried with my people?'

Another more practical proposal is 'Live in my heart and pay no rent.'

Before the age of fifty-five there is no such thing as a confirmed bachelor, only an obstinate one.

The best test of a man is his choice of a wife.

Blind men and deaf women have the most successful marriages.

Donegal girls have been given a special dispensation by the pope to wear the thick part of their legs below their knees.

It is better to be quarrelling than lonely.

A poor man should always marry young, so that he will have plenty of children to take care of him in his old age.

If you marry the right woman there is nothing like it; and if you marry the wrong woman there is nothing like it.

The women of Ireland have
always come first.

When a man is born, people
ask, 'How is the mother?'

When a man marries, people
admire the bride.

When a man dies, people ask, 'How much did he
leave her?'

A family from Kerry was delighted when the
matchmaker found the daughter of a rich Waterford
farmer for the handsome but penniless eldest son.
When he saw his bride, however, the young man
turned her down.

'What's wrong with her?' said her father.

'Begob, she's lame,' said he.

'And what's that to it?' said the father. 'Surely
you're not wanting her for racing?'

The only thing better than a good wife is no wife.

During the Napoleonic Wars the many Irish officers
in the British army were particularly popular among
the ladies of London society. When an Irish farmer's
wife was chided by a friend for not educating her
second son for one of the professions, she dismissed
the criticism with, 'Ah, sure he's a good-looking boy.
When he's grown to manhood, I'll put him in a red
coat and send him to London and some rich English
lady can treat herself to him.'

A defendant in a Wexford court once declared, 'I've had seven sons and I've never raised my hand to any of them except in self-defence.'

It is a great pleasure entirely to be alone, especially when your sweetheart is with you.

Father Healy once offered sympathy to a parishioner with a black eye and asked who had hit her.

'Himself,' said she triumphantly. 'And who better?'

The young men of Ireland are not always as confident with women as their glib tongues might suggest. After a long courtship, a shy young farmer was heard saying to his sweetheart, 'I've eight more acres now and twelve more cows and I've built two new rooms on to the little house. If I were you, Mary, I would consider how comfortable I might be if I were to move there.'

'Ah Tom,' said she with wide eyes and a smile, 'if I were you and you were me, I'd have been married years ago.'

A charitable lady from Dublin was calling on houses in the streets of Dalkey. 'I am collecting for the new home for drunkards,' she said to the woman who answered the door.

'Right you are,' said the mistress of the house. 'Come back half an hour after closing time and you can have him.'

The following conversation was overheard in Phoenix Park:

'Do you dream of me, Michael?'

'Ah Kate, my darlin', I can't sleep for dreamin' of ye.'

Wives always outlast their dowries.

A rich farmer with an ugly daughter can always make her pretty with cows.

A farmer went into a bank in Tralee and asked to make a deposit of £200. 'It's from my wife's estate,' said he. 'She died yesterday.'

The manager looked at him curiously. 'Don't I remember you making a deposit of a few hundred from your wife's estate a year ago?'

'Ah indeed you do, your honour,' said the farmer. 'That was my first wife. I'm very lucky with women.'

Marry in haste, repent at leisure.

It is a foolish woman that knows a foolish man's faults.

A party of English tourists in Killarney at the end of the last century recorded the following candid admission by their guide. 'When I was courtin' herself, I was that fond of her I could have eaten her. But today, by God, I wish I had, for I've had to swallow a lot since then.'

An Irish dairy maid once attempted to explain the
difference between English and Irish marriages to the
wife of the English resident magistrate. 'When an
Irish wife has words with her husband, she can end
up in bed with a black eye. But when an English wife
goes and does it, she can end up in bed alone.'

FOOD AND DRINK

♣

A traveller from England arrived long after midnight at a tavern on a remote part of the coast of County Clare and found to his delight that it was still open. He ordered a drink and then said to the landlord, 'When do you close?'

'Oh, I should think around the end of November.'

A woman buying a lobster in a Bray fishmonger's handed it back and complained that it only had one claw.

'There are a lot like that,' said the fishmonger. 'They lose them in fights.'

'How much is it for a winner, then?'

A well-known doctor in Wexford was summoned to the house of a farmer who, he found to his surprise, was suffering from pneumonia. The farmer was unable to explain it. 'I went to the fair at Enniscorthy yesterday and when it was over I walked home and when I got home I took off my hat and

trousers and hung them on the back of the door and went to bed, and then when I woke up I was lying in a ditch full of water and my hat and trousers were hanging from a tree.'

Whiskey bottles have narrow necks to stop Irishmen from knocking off the contents in one go.

There's many a drunk outlived a doctor.

A Dublin drayman once pleaded that he was unfit for work because he had been to a christening the day before and 'the baby was the only one there that took water'.

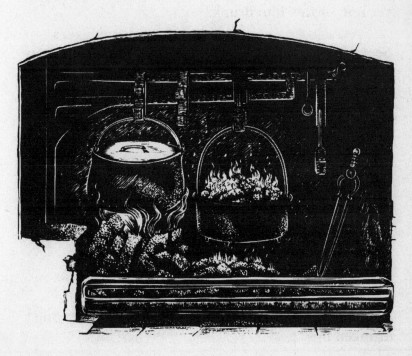

Never take one for the road
until you know where
the road is.

Two Tipperary
farm labourers
were overheard discussing the eminent and dignified
judge who had recently bought the estate on which
they worked.

'He is very rich entirely,' said one. 'He has a
hundred pounds a quarter, maybe.'

'Ah no,' said the other, 'he has a hundred a week,
if he has a shilling.'

'Glory to God, as much as that,' said the first. 'And
yet I never saw him drunk.'

Seeing a parishioner staggering out of a bar yet again
and weaving down the village street, a priest called
out to him in warning, 'That's a long, hard, unhappy
road you've set yourself out on, Michael.'

'Ah, sure it's not that that bothers me, Father,' said
the spinning drunkard. 'It's the bloody width of it.'

'Are you telling the court that you only had one glass
of whiskey?' asked the resident magistrate.

'Yes, sir.'

'And where did you have it?'

'Oh, in many different places, your honour.'

A secret buried in a sober heart can come to life on
drunken lips.

The Irish artist and author
Robert Gibbings, whose
works adorn these pages,
was an enormous man.
One day a tiny
woman walked up
to him in his native
Cork and said, 'Begob,
sir, you make great use of your food.'

Nobody ever had to found a charity for needy
publicans.

Sir Frederick Flood was a member of a delegation of
Irish Protestants who went to London at the
beginning of the nineteenth century to meet the
Prime Minister, William Pitt. As often happened in
those days, the conversation at dinner turned to the
Irish capacity for alcohol, an accomplishment for
which the English had a grudging admiration.

'Do you tell me, Sir Frederick,' said Pitt, 'that you
can drink five bottles of claret without any help?'

'Oh, no,' said Sir Frederick. 'I have the help of a
bottle of port.'

Whiskey is a cure for everything but
sadness.

After being repeatedly solicited for his
custom by a Dublin wine merchant,
an eighteenth-century Wicklow

gentleman who was a legendary consumer of claret wrote the following letter to the merchant:

My dear sir,

I am not rich enough to pay for your wine myself, but I should be very happy to serve you in another way. If you will send me a list of your best customers, I shall endeavour to cultivate their acquaintance.

The drink has found husbands for many a spinster.

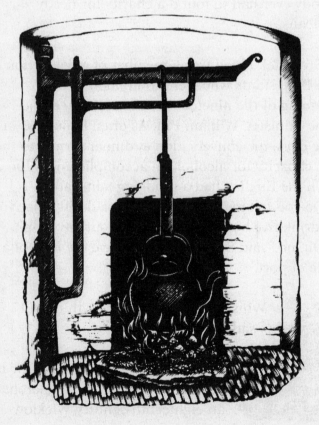

'You have told this court that you regularly drink four and twenty tumblers of whiskey punch. Do you swear to that?' said prosecuting counsel. 'Did you ever drink five and twenty?'

'I am on oath,' said the witness, 'and I'll swear no further than that, for I never kept count beyond the two dozen.'

The great Irish playwright Richard Brinsley Sheridan served as a member in many of the same Parliaments as the famous evangelical reformer and abolitionist William Wilberforce. Early one morning while making his way home from one of the fashionable clubs, Sheridan succumbed to the effects of brandy, sat down in St James's Street and went to sleep with his head against a wall. He awoke an hour or so later to find three big Bow Street Runners standing round him, prodding him with their boots and asking his name. 'I am a member of Parliament,' said 'Sherry'. 'My name is William Wilberforce.'

On another occasion, as the evening was beginning, Sheridan asked the assembled company if they intended to drink like men or beasts.

'Like men,' came the unanimous reply.

'Good,' said Sheridan. 'Then we shall get drunk. Only beasts know when they have had enough.'

It has long been said that the people of Ireland only became poor when the devil invented Scotch whisky.

Few are the friendships that have not been forged over a bottle.

DEATH

♣

If the rich could pay people to die for them, the poor would make a marvellous living.

Even the candlemaker dies in the dark.

The birds and beasts are frightened by dying; only men are afraid of death.

The actor and playwright Joseph Tomelty used to say that if there was music in hell it was the bagpipes.

A letter to the Irish Times recorded the following incident outside a Dublin Bingo hall. As a funeral approached, a woman left the queue that was waiting for the hall to open, knelt down in the street and prayed until the coffin had passed. When she rejoined the queue, the writer heard the woman next to her asking why she had done it.

'And why shouldn't I,' said she. 'Wasn't he a good husband to me?'

There'll be few at the funeral if you die in harvest time.

When an old woman in County Limerick was on her deathbed, her grandchildren tried to persuade her to be buried in the new graveyard in the village instead of with her husband in Kileely thirty miles away.

'I will not,' said she. 'I would never be comfortable without another bone or a pinch of dust belonging to me. Take me to Kileely and let me lie among decent Christians.'

There are more tears at the wake if the corpse was rich.

When the famous Irish clown Johnny Patterson was on his deathbed, the doctor tried to appear optimistic by leaving quickly with a cheerful 'I'll see you in the morning, Johnny'.

'Sure you will, doc,' said the clown. 'But will I see you?'

The last whispered words of the playwright Brendan Behan, to the nun who had nursed him for several days: 'May you be the mother of a bishop.'

During one of the many long, frightening lulls in the fighting in the First World War, an English officer said to the Irish soldier in the trench beside him,

'If the devil could take only one of us now, which do you think he would pick?'

'Oh, he'd take me for sure,' said the Irishman.

'Why do you say that?' said the officer.

'Ah, sure he knows he can have you any time.'

There is no need for a wall round a cemetery. The people inside can't get out and the people outside don't want to get in.

There are more lies told at a wake than in court.

When his grim physician told him that he was about to die, Queen Victoria's merry Irish Prime Minister Lord Palmerston muttered, 'Die, my dear doctor. That is the last thing I shall do.'

A Dublin woman once reported the state of her mother's health ambiguously: 'She was at death's door yesterday, but the doctor pulled her through.'

When the much-loved Father Healy of Bray was on his deathbed, knowing that the end was near, news was brought to him that one of his oldest and closest friends was in the same peril. 'I am afraid it is going to be a dead heat,' he said.

The patriot, advocate and orator John Philpot Curran had more than his share of trouble and sadness. His tongue landed him in five duels, his wife ran away with a clergyman, his daughter died of a broken heart after the execution of her lover, Robert Emmet, and his own heart was almost broken by the Act of Union. But he kept his wit and his levity to the end. A few days before his death, his doctor made what had become a regular morning visit and remarked that he was coughing very badly. 'That's surprising,' said Curran. 'I've been practising all night.'

When told on his deathbed that he had built up a huge medical bill, Oscar Wilde said, 'Ah, well then, I suppose that I shall have to die beyond my means.'

The following exchange was overheard by an anonymous priest at a funeral in Castlebar.

'I blame the doctors, Kathleen. A healthy man like himself should never have died so suddenly. Their diagnosis must have been wrong.'

'Oh no indeed,' said the grieving widow. 'They were right entirely. When I took him to the hospital they told me he would be out within a week and he was.'

THE REPARTEE

♣

A teacher at one of the most exclusive private schools in Dublin was still talking when the bell rang to signal the end of the lesson. At once the boys began to pack up their books and leave. 'Just one more moment, if you please,' said he. 'I still have a few more pearls to cast.'

In the 1890s, when the advocates of the many temperance societies were legion on the streets of Dublin, an ancient citizen was stopped by one of them as he was entering a bar. 'Do you realize, my friend,' said the good campaigner, 'that if you go in there the devil goes with you?'

'Well he needn't bother,' said the sinner, 'for I have only tuppence on me.'

Among these advocates of temperance there was none more ardent than a Member of Parliament called A M Sullivan. One day, while walking in the Wicklow Mountains, he slipped and sprained his ankle.

His local guide produced a flask of whiskey and gently rubbed some into the swelling. Within minutes Sullivan was on his feet and walking again. 'Faith, there you are, sir,' said the guide. 'It would be a long time before soda water could do that for you.'

A Victorian tourist wrote a letter to a London newspaper describing a visit to the west of Ireland, on which he had one day met a young farmer driving cattle to a fair. When he met the farmer again in the evening he asked him how much he had got for his stock.

'Four pounds a head,' said the farmer.

'Only four pounds a head,' said the Englishman. 'Why, if you took them to my county of Hampshire in England, you could get at least six pounds a head for them.'

'Oh I don't doubt that, your honour,' said the farmer. 'If I could take the lakes of Killarney to Purgatory, I could charge a pound a drop for them.'

A farm manager near Clonmel was hiring casual labour for the harvest. 'I am afraid you're too small,' said he to one of the most eager applicants.

'Begob sir, why's that,' said the wee man in astonishment. 'Do you cut your corn at the top or what?'

A dignified Protestant clergyman was approached by a beggar in Cork. 'For the blessing of God, could your honour spare me a coin?'

'I will not give money to anyone who appeals to me like that,' said the reverend gentleman. 'But what I will give you is valuable advice: do not take the name of God in vain.'

'In vain is it?' said the beggar. 'And whose fault is that I'd like to know?'

The clergyman became even more affronted. 'I think you ought to be asking for manners not money.'

'Ah, sure I asked for what I thought your honour had most of.'

The Irish beggar's reputation for wit is well deserved. At the end of the last century, a splendidly dressed footman in Stephen's Green, Dublin, was heard shouting at a beggar, 'Get along with you and take your rags with you.'

'Never you mind my clothes, my good man,' said the poor wretch with the greatest dignity. 'At least they are my own.'

While collecting material for his Irish Sketch Book, the English novelist William Makepeace Thackeray decided to take a pinch of snuff just as he was approaching a beggar-woman on a country road. Seeing him put his hand into his pocket, the woman cried out, 'May the blessing of God follow your honour all your life.' But when all he did was to take out his snuff box and walk on past her, she added more loudly, 'And may it never catch up with you.'

A medical specialist in London's fashionable Harley Street at the end of the last century recounted the story of an Irish farmer who had spent his savings on consulting him. While writing down some details about his patient, the specialist asked whether the male members of his family were long-lived. 'Well now,' said the farmer, 'it's difficult to say. I'm from Galway. The longevity of my ancestors has been entirely dependent on the fluctuating benevolence of juries.'

Wit develops early in Ireland. A rich gentleman, noted for his elegance, told how he was walking across O'Connell Bridge finishing a fine cigar when two urchins ran up behind him shouting, 'Throw us the butt, sir. Go on, sir, give us the butt.'

The gentleman ignored them and continued on his way; and a few moments later he heard one say loudly to the other, 'Ah, leave him. He'll not part with it. Sure, it's only a butt he's picked up himself.'

In a bar in the sea-side resort of Kilkee in County Clare, an English tourist was patronizing the supposedly simple peasantry, much to the amusement of his chortling companions. 'Come now,' said he to the little man with string round his trousers who was standing along the bar from him. 'Tell us the biggest lie you've ever told and I'll buy you a pint for it.'

'Oh, that's kind indeed,' said the little man. 'By my soul, your honour is a perfect gentleman.'

Another English tourist was being shown round the Galtee Mountains early in the last century. His guide pointed to a gap in the hills. 'That's called the Devil's Bit,' he said, 'and the low hill hard by it is the Devil's Chair.'

'The devil seems to own a good deal of property in these parts,' said the tourist.

'Oh indeed he does, sir,' said the guide, 'but like most landlords he lives in England.'

After the death of a popular Dublin doctor, who, like many fashionable physicians, had made a great deal more money than his true ability merited, a group of friends gathered to discuss an appropriate inscription for his huge headstone in Mount Jerome cemetery. Eventually someone suggested that they should use the same inscription as had been used for Sir Christopher Wren in his great masterpiece, St Paul's Cathedral:

Si monumentum requiris circumspice
If you seek his monument, look about you

At the beginning of this century, an amateur English orator was attacking the Irish Home Rule movement from his soap box at Speakers' Corner in Hyde Park in London. Noticing that he had a wooden leg, an old Irish soldier in the crowd, who had himself lost an arm in the service of Britain, asked him how he had lost the limb. The speaker turned on him with a sneer. 'On examining my pedigree, I discovered that I had some Irish blood in me; and being convinced that it had settled in my left foot, I had the leg amputated at once.'

'Ah, is that right,' said the soldier. 'It's a pity it didn't settle in your head.'

Lady Carteret, the wife of the Lord Lieutenant of Ireland, told Dean Jonathan Swift, 'The air in your country is healthy and very excellent.'

'For God's sake, madam,' said Swift, 'don't say so in England. If you do, they will certainly tax it.'

Swift himself once proposed that there should be a tax on female beauty. When someone suggested that women would never pay enough to make the tax worth levying, Swift answered, 'That would be the least of our worries. Let every woman be permitted to assess her own charms, then she'll be generous enough.'

Novelist, poet and playwright Oliver Goldsmith said that the true use of speech was not so much to express our wants as to conceal them.

Goldsmith also said that the wise are polite all the world over, but fools are only polite at home.

At a literary gathering in London, an author greeted Goldsmith as 'the greatest living writer in English' and declared himself unworthy to be called even a hack in the presence of so great an artist.

'How dare he?' said Goldsmith after he had walked away. 'He's not important enough to humble himself like that.'

Dr Samuel Johnson recorded a charming
story about Goldsmith. Johnson was at
home one day when a messenger
came with a note from Goldsmith
asking for the immediate loan of a guinea;
his landlady was threatening to evict him
and he needed the money to pay off at least part
of his overdue rent. Johnson gave the messenger the
guinea and followed him soon afterwards to
Goldsmith's lodgings. In the Irishman's little room
there was a large pile of manuscript on the table.
When Johnson asked what it was, he was told that it
was a recently completed novel, *The Vicar of Wakefield*.
After reading a few pages he persuaded Goldsmith to
let him take it round to the publisher Francis Newbery;
and before the day was over he had returned with an
advance of sixty guineas.

'Why did you not sell the book when you needed
money?' he asked as they sat down to a celebration
dinner.

'I didn't think of it,' said Goldsmith.

'But why do you write if not for money?'

'I don't know, but whatever the reason I certainly
don't do it for avaricious landladies.'

In 1776 no less, Myles MacDermott, Prince of
Coolavin, the head of one of the most ancient and
noble families in Ireland, was invited to a grand
dinner which was being given by the British Lord
Lieutenant in Dublin Castle. Arriving a little late after
a long journey, he took his place quietly at the foot of

the table. Seeing this, the Lord Lieutenant sent one of his *aides-de-camp* to invite the prince to sit beside him at the head of the table. But the young officer's jaw dropped at the reply. 'Tell his Excellency that wherever the MacDermott sits is the head of the table.'

When one of Richard Brinsley Sheridan's many creditors asked him to pay at least the interest on his debt, the playwright replied, 'My dear fellow, it is not in my interest to pay the principle or in my principle to pay the interest.'

Two drunk and stupid English lords decided to taunt Sheridan at a reception at Brighton Pavilion. 'Tell us, sir,' said one of them, 'Which are you – a fool or a rogue?'

Sheridan took each one by the arm and began to stroll across the room. 'Well gentlemen,' said he, 'at the moment I am between the two.'

On 24 February 1809, news was brought to the House of Commons that Sheridan's new theatre in Drury Lane was on fire. Lord Temple suggested that the House should adjourn, but Sheridan, who was then Member for the English constituency of Stafford, insisted calmly that 'whatever might be the extent of the calamity', it was not enough to merit interrupting the proceedings. He even waited himself until the debate was over before setting out for the theatre. Soon afterwards a few friends followed him and found to their horror that he was ruined. The building for which he had run up enormous debts was blazing beyond salvation.

On asking where they might find the owner, they were directed to the Piazza Coffee House opposite. There, in the window, sat Sheridan, a glass in his hand and a bottle of claret on the table beside him. He was as composed as ever, and when one of the company remarked upon it in admiration, the tragic hero smiled. 'A man may surely take a glass of wine by his own fireside.'

Lord Lauderdale, who was famously long-winded and boring, once cornered Sheridan and announced that he was about to tell him 'a most amusing story'.

'Oh, please, no,' said Sheridan. 'A joke in your mouth is no laughing matter.'

Michael Kelly, who wrote derivative tunes and sold second-rate wine, asked Sheridan to help him write a slogan that would advertise both his trades above his shop in St James's. After a moment's thought, Sheridan came up with this simple suggestion: 'Michael Kelly, composer of wine and importer of music'.

Daniel O'Connell once described a particularly stiff and formal lady in Dublin society as having all the characteristics of a poker, with the exception of its occasional warmth.

On being introduced into a Dublin drawing room filled with self-important nonentities, the great John Philpot Curran was informed by an awe-struck friend that every man in the room came from a noble family and had several distinguished ancestors. 'Bless my soul,' said Curran, 'a crowd of anti-climaxes.'

Curran was never impressed by people who took themselves too seriously. He once described a particularly reserved and over-dignified gentleman as 'afraid to smile lest anyone might suppose that he was too familiar with himself'.

Curran was once bested by no less a person than the lovable Sir Boyle Roche, who was by no means as simple as his many endearing 'bulls' made him out to be. In answer to a reproach in the Irish House of Commons, Curran had declared that he was the guardian of his own honour. At this, Sir Boyle rose to express his surprise. 'On other occasions,' he said, 'I have heard the Honourable gentleman declare that he is the enemy of sinecures.'

Curran and a friend were walking through Dublin when they met an acquaintance who had the thickest of Kerry accents. 'By God,' said the friend after they had moved on, 'that man murders the English language.'

'Oh, I wouldn't say that,' said Curran. 'All that he does is knock an 'i' out.'

One of Ireland's few dull and studious lawyers was showing Chief Baron O'Grady over the large and very secluded library which he had just built for himself on the end of one wing of his country house. 'This is splendid,' said O'Grady. 'My dear fellow, you could study here from morning to midnight and no one on earth would be any the wiser.'

In Ireland, as elsewhere, in the nineteenth century, a fine library was one of the most important status symbols among the newly rich. One such gentleman was showing the library in his expensive new house to a group of guests which included Father James Healy. 'And here,' said he, waving a hand pretentiously at the shelves, 'surrounded by these best friends, I am always at my happiest.'

'And you are a true friend to them as well,' said Father Healy, turning one of the volumes over in his hand, 'for I see that you never cut or use them.'

When Earl Spencer was Lord Lieutenant, Father Healy was a regular dinner guest at Viceregal Lodge and Dublin Castle. On one occasion the Earl and

several others were discussing Renaissance religious painting and the Earl remarked that as far as he knew there were two kinds of angels, Cherubim and Seraphim, but that he could not for the life of him remember what the difference was. One of his *aides-de-camp* suggested that Father Healy should know, and Earl Spencer instructed the young man to ask him.

'What is it?' said Healy, who had been talking to one of the other guests.

'We wondered what the difference was between Cherubim and Seraphim,' said the ADC.

'Well now,' said the Father, 'I believe there was a difference between them a long time ago. But I am glad to say that they have since made it up.'

At the end of the last century there was a famous major-domo at the Lord Mayor's Mansion House in Dublin who was known as 'Old White'. One day when the Lord Mayor was admonishing him for yet another neglect of duty, White said, 'Does your lordship really believe that I would do a thing like that?'

'Certainly,' said the Lord Mayor. 'I have heard it from several members of the Corporation.'

'Begob,' said White, 'if I believed all that those boys said about you, I wouldn't think you fit to be Lord Mayor of Dublin.'

According to the Nationalist professor of economics Tom Kettle, ideas are like umbrellas. 'If left lying about, they are peculiarly liable to a change of ownership.'

Kettle also said that the most important thing at a public dinner was not the menu but the man that you had to sit next to.

The novelist Charles Lever, whose brother was a priest, was visiting Dr Whately, the Archbishop of Dublin. While walking in the garden, the archbishop plucked a leaf from a rare plant in his collection. Remarking that the plant was well known among botanists for having a particularly nauseating flavour, he asked one of the obsequious priests who walked behind him to try it. The unfortunate priest took the leaf obediently, bit into it and screwed up his face in an appropriately revolted expression. The archbishop pulled another leaf. 'You try it, Lever.'

'Thank you, no,' said Lever. 'My brother is not in your Grace's diocese.'

The poet William Butler Yeats was also manager of the Abbey Theatre. One day, after many frustrating attempts to get the lighting right for a sunset scene, a deep red glow appeared suddenly along the back of the stage. 'That's it,' cried Yeats. 'That's exactly what I want.'

The head of his electrician appeared slowly through the trap door in the centre of the stage. 'Well you can't have it. The bloody theatre's on fire.'

According to Yeats, his father, the artist John Butler Yeats, used to say that the great difference between England and Ireland was that all Englishmen had rich relations and all Irishmen poor ones.

On meeting Yeats for the first time at his fortieth birthday party, James Joyce said, 'We have met too late Mr Yeats. You are too old to be influenced by me.'

One morning at breakfast, James Joyce's father told his wife that the newspaper contained an obituary of an old friend.

'Oh, don't tell me that Mrs. Cassidy is dead,' said she.

'Well, I don't know about that,' said he, 'but somebody has taken the liberty of burying her.'

As a young man Oscar Wilde once stopped a student in the gate of Trinity College, Dublin, and invited him to come home with him to Merrion Square. 'I want to introduce you to my mother,' he said. 'We have founded a society for the suppression of virtue.'

'I choose my friends for their good looks, my acquaintances for their good characters, and my enemies for their intellects. A man cannot be too careful,' said Oscar Wilde, 'in the choice of his enemies.'

'Experience', said Wilde, 'is the name which everyone gives to his mistakes.'

On being asked if he knew the author George Moore, Wilde replied, 'Yes, I know him so well that I have not spoken to him for ten years.'

The statesman and philosopher
Arthur Balfour asked Wilde
what his religion was. 'Well,
you know, I don't think
I have any,' said Wilde.
'I am an Irish Protestant.'

Wilde excused his expensive lifestyle by saying, 'It is a
duty we owe to the dignity of letters.'

Lord Avebury, who had published a list of his
'hundred best books', asked Wilde at a dinner party
if he could compile a list of his hundred favourites.
    'I am afraid that would be impossible,' said Wilde.
    'Why is that?'
    'Because I have only written five.'

'Bernard Shaw', said Wilde, 'is an excellent man. He has
not an enemy in the world and none of his friends like him.'

In talking about America, Wilde said that it had often
been discovered before Columbus, but the discovery
had always been hushed up.

On his visit to the United States, Wilde was asked by
a reporter why he always carried a huge fur coat with
him. 'To hide the hideous sofas in all the hotel rooms.'

On being invited by some citizens of Griggsville to
lecture them on aesthetics, Wilde answered, 'Begin by
changing the name of your town.'

Wilde described American girls as 'little oases of pretty unreasonableness in a vast desert of practical common sense'.

On hearing that the English poet and painter Dante Gabriel Rosetti had given an impoverished poet enough money to go to America in order to put an end to his constant cadging, Wilde said, 'Of course, if one had the money to go to America, one would not go.'

Oscar Wilde was as witty in conversation as he was in his writing. Here are just a few more examples:

I sometimes think that God in creating man somewhat overestimated his ability.

Always forgive your enemies. Nothing annoys them so much.

Crying is the refuge of plain women and the ruin of pretty ones.

She who hesitates is won.

No man is rich enough to buy back his past.

A gentleman is one who never hurts anyone's feelings unintentionally.

A poet can survive anything but a misprint.

After the first performance of one of his plays, George Bernard Shaw went on to the stage to receive rapturous applause. When at last it died down, a man

in the gallery began to boo and hiss. 'I quite agree with you, my friend,' said Shaw. 'It is a rotten play. But who are we among so many?'

Asked by a reporter why he had a long flowing beard, Shaw replied that he had grown it out of vanity but that he kept it out of common sense.

'How is that?' asked the reporter.

'Well,' said Shaw, 'in all those years, I have probably written several plays in the time that I would have spent shaving.'

At a London dinner party the famous dancer Isadora Duncan suggested to Shaw that they ought to get married and produce a wonderful child with her body and his brains.

'I am flattered,' said Shaw, 'but I am afraid I must decline. The child might not be so lucky. It might have your brains and my body.'

The fat newspaper tycoon Lord Northcliffe once attempted to mock Shaw's lean figure. 'The trouble with you, Shaw', he said, 'is that you always look as if there was a famine in the land.'

'The trouble with you, Northcliffe', said Shaw, 'is that you always look as though you were the cause of it.'

An ambitious London hostess who had never met him once presumed to send Shaw an invitation to an 'at home' on such and such a date. A couple of days later she received the simple reply 'Bernard Shaw likewise'.

'A coquette', said Shaw, 'is a woman who arouses passions she has no intention of gratifying.'

On a more serious subject, Shaw also said that 'if all economists were laid end to end, they would not reach a conclusion'.

'Americans adore me,' said Shaw, 'and they will go on adoring me until I say something nice about them.'

A young man in New York asked John McCormack how to become a great tenor.

'Begin with ballads,' said McCormack.

'But you were singing arias at the age of ten,' said the young man.

'Yes,' said McCormack, 'but I didn't ask how.'

The hostess at a London cocktail party made the mistake of asking the playwright Brendan Behan if he had been talking to 'lots of interesting people'.

'Not yet,' said Behan, 'but I've only been here two hours.'

When Behan was at the height of his fame, a man went up to him in a Dublin bar and asked him for the loan of five pounds. When Behan refused, the man became haughty. 'I can remember the time when you had nothing.'

'That may be,' said Behan, 'but you don't remember it half as well as I do.'

THE COUNTRY LIFE

❧

The wrath of God is nothing to the wrath of an Irishman outbid on a horse.

The possessions dearest to an Irishman's heart are land and horses.

There is nothing but the grace of God between the saddle and the ground.

The last horse home blames the bit.

A good man feeds his beasts before he sits to his own dinner.

This is a true story, recorded by the priest who took part in the incident and widely believed to be the origin of a joke which has been used by almost every comedian the world over in the last two hundred years.

Up until almost the end of the eighteenth

century, it was the custom in Ireland for the boys and girls of a village to meet well away from any buildings for a bit of illicit dancing at the crossroads. And it was usual on these occasions, if it was at all possible, to employ a blind fiddler, so that any indiscretions or improprieties could not be observed.

On one such occasion, outside the village of Ballygriffin, near Cashel, the fiddler was playing the fine jig 'The Cat's Rambles to the Child's Saucepan' when the dancers noticed their parish priest, Father Barrett, advancing across the fields. By the time Father Barrett reached the crossroads, the fiddler, although still playing, was alone.

'What are you doing, man?' bellowed Barrett. 'Do you not know the Third Commandment?'

The fiddler stopped playing and scratched his head. 'It sounds familiar enough, but I can't recall it. Maybe if you whistled a bar or two, it might come back to me.'

A group of Victorian tourists from England and America went to visit the Wicklow Mountains in a horse-drawn car. They were so engrossed in conversation that they were oblivious to the breathtaking scenery and quite unaware that the car was moving slower and slower as the poor horse struggled up a steep hill.

Eventually
the driver
jumped down
to lessen the
weight and
walked along
beside the
horse. Then, after
they had gone a few
hundred yards, he
stopped the car, went
back to one of the doors,
opened it and slammed it, and then moved the horse
on again. After another few hundred yards, he did
the same thing. When he did it for a third time, one
of his passengers stuck his head out of the window
and asked what he was doing.

'I'm foolin' the horse,' said he. 'Each time I slam
the door, he thinks one of you lot has got out and he
sets to work with new heart.'

A son's chair in his father's house is sturdy and well
cushioned. A father's stool in his son's house is always
low and hard.

There's many a farm that grew bigger through the
lace of a daughter's petticoat.

When asked how many his jaunting car could hold,
the Killarney driver replied, 'Four if you sit
contagious and six if you sit familiar.'

The tallest flowers hide the fiercest nettles.

An English lady travelling in Galway in the middle of the last century recorded meeting a beggar woman on a lonely road who said to her, 'For the love of God, my lady, give us a crust of bread, for I am so thirsty I don't know where I'll sleep tonight.'

Never kill a cricket on your hearth. His family will eat your socks.

The wine cellars at Castle Hacket in Galway never run out of wine. No matter how many unexpected guests there are or how long they stay, they can be served indefinitely with the finest Spanish wine.

In the early Middle Ages, when the Spaniards first shipped their wine to the west coast of Ireland, the leaders of the Kirwan family, who were even then lords of Castle Hacket, always left out a few kegs at night for Finvarra, King of the western fairies. The custom has continued over the centuries ever since, and in return for the kindness, Finvarra has always ensured that the castle's own supply is inexhaustible.

A man was fishing on the end of the pier at Dunlaoghlaire

when an English tourist asked him, 'What sort of fish do you catch here, my man?'

'Well, sir,' said the fisherman, 'you can never tell till you get them up.'

A woman crying is as hard a sight to any heart as a bare-footed duck.

A farmer from Kerry went to look at some land in the much lusher neighbouring county of Limerick. He saw several fields that suited him, but the rent was too much and the landlord would not come down. 'This land is not like your miserable Kerry land,' said the landlord. 'The grass here grows so fast and high that if you left a heifer in that field for the night you would scarcely find her in the morning.'

'Well now,' said the Kerryman without the slightest surprise. 'There's many a part of Kerry where if you were fool enough to leave a heifer out at night there's devil the bit of her you'd ever see again.'

More men have caught
colds from damp fancy
clothes than from the sweat of
their brows.

It's better to own a little than
to want a lot.

The best knitting is done
after dark, because the sheep are asleep.

A country gentleman admonished a man for begging
when there was plenty of work in the hayfields. 'Ah,
we can't all work,' said the beggar. 'If we did, there'd
be nothing for the rest to do.'

Hold on to the bone and the dog will follow.

A hungry dog will eat dirty puddings.

A man who doesn't spend when he's single will never
give when he's not.

The women in Tyrone will never buy a rabbit without
a head on it, in case it turns out to be a cat.

There are enough twigs on every tree to burn it.

Stones and mortar make a house, but a home needs
the laughter of children.

If there's none in
the house with work
or land, there'll not
be enough to baptize
a fairy.

Cast not a clout till May be out.

A child that has never lived in the country has only
had half a childhood.

Dance with the girl that has the looks, but marry the
one with the farm.

The south wind is soft and mild,
And is very good for the seeds.

The north wind is cold, and when
It blows the lambs are born.

The west wind is a generous wind
And fills the fishermen's nets.

The east wind is dark and gloomy
And is the harbinger of frost.

Red in the South means rain and cold.

Red in the east a sign of frost.

Red in the north rain and wind.

Red in the west sunshine and thaw.

An English gentleman who visited Ireland on
government business at the end of the eighteenth
century recorded the following incident as the
epitome of Irish country life. While travelling through
County Limerick, he was invited to dine in the house
of an Irish gentleman whom he had never met before.
After consuming vast quantities of claret and almost
as many bottles of port, the assembled company got
down to the serious drinking of whiskey punch,
which was made with the help of a huge old kettle
which an ancient servant filled at the well in front of
the house. Shortly before midnight, as the ancient
servant set out to fill a second kettle, the English
gentleman took his leave, pleading that he had to rise
early for a long journey.

After a few hours' sleep, the English gentleman
breakfasted at his inn, climbed into his carriage and
set out on the king's business. As he passed the house
where he had dined, the candles were still burning in
the great hall, laughter was still spilling through the
open windows, and in the grey first light of day the
ancient servant could be seen limping back to the
house from the well with yet another kettle.

The Irish are the only people to have discovered that
horses can talk.

In the old days the butlers in Irish country
houses were a separate breed with
little of the tact and diffidence that
distinguished their English counterparts.

An English visitor to Castletown House reported the following answer to her enquiry from the ancient retainer who met her at the door. 'Physically speaking, her ladyship is indeed at home, but whether she is or not to you is something that I will have to go up and find out.'

On being summoned to give the last rites to a farmer, Father Dennis McMahon of Tuam arrived to find the old man still putting his affairs in order with his solicitor. The voice from the deathbed was a feeble whisper, 'There's three that still owes me money. Murphy owes me fifty pound for the horse. Kelly owes me five for milk. And O'Gorman still owes me sixteen for last summer's barley.'

'Ah, God, what a fine man he is,' said the weeping wife in the chair beside him. 'Would you listen to that. He's lucid to the end.'

But the whisper from the bed continued, 'And that should be more than enough for the sixty-five I owe McConnell.'

'Ah, merciful Jesus, the pity of it,' said the wife. 'Pay no mind to him. The poor man's raving at last.'

The following advertisement appeared in the personal column of the Newtownards Chronicle.

'Lost: a cameo brooch representing Venus and Adonis on the Bangor Road at about midnight last Thursday.'

On becoming Ireland's first cultural attaché to Mexico at the end of the 1920s, Francis Dooley recorded that he felt completely at home after the following incident:

Appalled by the fact that most Mexican men travelled on the backs of mules while their long-suffering wives walked in the dust beside them, Dooley at last found the courage to ask one of them why. 'Because', came the answer, 'my wife does not own a mule.'

THE PROVERBS

The road to hell is paved with good intentions.

The road to Heaven is well signposted, but it is badly lit at night.

Never trust anyone who doesn't like cats.

Any man who owns a cow can always find a woman to milk her.

He who pays the piper calls the tune.

No rearing, no manners.

The blacksmith's horse and the cobbler's wife are always the last to have shoes.

No matter how tall your grandfather was, you have to do your own growing.

Don't bid the devil good day till you meet him.

The tongue ties knots that the teeth cannot loosen.

If it's got badly, it'll go badly.

Castles were built a stone at a time.

You can't build a barrel round a bung hole.

Never ask a fox to mind the hens.

The English always credit the rest of us with the qualities they don't need themselves.

If you lend your coat, don't cut off the buttons.

There are as many good fish in the sea as ever came out of it.

The smaller the cabin the wider the door.

There's as many good horses in carts as in coaches.

Never buy bread from a butcher.

A windy day is the wrong one for thatching.

Even black hens lay white eggs.

It is better to be born lucky than rich.

Trouble hates nothing as much as a smile.

Constant company wears out its welcome.

Never sleep with a stranger or borrow from a neighbour.

If the cat had a dowry, she would often be kissed.

You can kill a dog more ways than by choking it with butter.

When a heifer is far from home she grows longer horns.

Even a tin knocker shines on a dirty door.

A golden ring can tie a man as tight as any chain.

Only the rich can afford compassion.

You can take a man out of the bog, but you can't take the bog out of the man.

A nod is as good as a wink to a blind donkey.

The best looking-glass is the eyes of a friend.

You can't teach an old dog new tricks.

There's a fool born every minute – and every one of them lives!

The heavier the purse, the lighter the heart.

Fair words never fed a friar.

If you don't want flour on your shoes, don't go into the mill.

You couldn't make half a football team out of all the Leinster men in Heaven.

Never call a Kerry man a fool until you're sure he's not a rogue.

There's many a good tune played on an old fiddle.

If you have a roving eye, it's no use having the other one fixed on Heaven.

There's little to choose between two blind goats.

Neighbours bring comfort in adversity but only envy in success.

Great mansions have slippery doorsteps.

God is good, but never dance in a small boat.

Be kind to those that you meet as you rise, you may pass them again as you fall.

Soft words butter no turnips.

A little dog can start a hare, but it takes a big one to catch it.

Big bellies were never generous.

There's many a ship lost within sight of harbour.

If a rogue deceives me once, shame on him. If he deceives me twice, shame on me.

All happy endings are beginnings as well.

There is a crock of gold in the tomb of every chieftain, but they are all guarded by cats and fairies.

The rabbit gets fat on what the hare misses.

It is the deaf people that create the lies.

The apple falls on the head that's under it.

A fool and his money are easily parted.

A man who holds good cards would never say if they were dealt wrong.

A ring on a good woman's finger is no good without a blouse on her back.

Discord is less painful than loneliness.

It is a lonely washing that has no man's shirt in it.

Never rub your eye with anything but your elbow.

There is not a tree in Heaven that is higher than the tree of patience.

If you don't know the way, walk slowly.

Limerick was, Dublin is, and Cork shall be The finest city of the three.

As honest as a cat when the meat is out of reach.

Reputations last longer than lives.

A man is no more encumbered by his soul than the steed by his bridle or the lake by the swan.

Only those who were born to hang are not afraid of water.

Big men are not the only kind that can reap a harvest.

Long loneliness is better than bad company.

There is no pain greater than the pain of rejection.

Idleness is a fool's desire.

The cat is always dignified, until the dog comes by.

The youngest thorns are the sharpest.

Never praise your son-in-law until the year is out.

Never give cherries to pigs or advice to fools.

A meeting in sunlight is lucky, and a burying in the rain.

A guest should be blind in another man's house.

A loud voice can make even the truth sound foolish.

There are three creatures beyond ruling – a mule, a pig and a woman.

It is a hard task to comfort the proud.

The beginning of a ship is a board, of a kiln a stone, of a king's reign salutation; and the beginning of health is sleep.

THE TRADITIONAL REMEDIES

♣

For deafness
One drop of fresh eel's oil every hour in each ear until
the patient begins to hear.
    The most effective oil is obtained by rolling the eel
in a cabbage leaf, putting it on the fire until it is soft
and then squeezing it.

Another useful ear-drop can be made by squeezing
the roots, leaves and blossom of cowslip in a linen
cloth and mixing the resulting juice with honey.

For rheumatism
Wear a copper or iron ring on the fourth finger of the
left hand.

For lethargy
Clear spirit, such as potheen,
sweetened with honey and
thickened with breadcrumbs
(this is also an excellent
remedy for a head cold).

For purifying the blood
Boiled carrot juice.

For sexual potency
Take two ounces of cochineal, one ounce of gentian root, two drachms of saffron, two drachms of snakeroot, two drachms of salt of wormwood and the rind of ten oranges, steep them for a few days in a quart of brandy and consume as required.

For preventing rabies after a bite from a mad dog
Take six ounces of rue, four ounces of garlic, two ounces of Venice treacle and two ounces of pewter filings, add two quarts of ale and boil for two hours in a covered pot. Strain before using and take a tablespoonful on an empty stomach every morning. (Venice treacle, now rare, is a mixture of over five dozen drugs in honey. If this cannot be found, ordinary treacle can be used instead, but the dosage must be increased.)

For lumbago
Take dog-fern roots and shamrocks, wash them and pound them and then mix them into a paste with butter and salt. Rub the mixture all over the back and leave it there until the lumbago is cured.

For liver complaints
Take the leaves of plantain, wild sage, shamrock and dock-leaf. Add valerian and the flower of the daisy. Boil them in a little water for an hour. Strain the liquor and drink a glassful twice a day.

For dysentery
Mix pounded woodbine with oatmeal, boil in milk and drink a glass three times a day.

For weak or tired eyes
Boil the flowers of daisies in a little water, allow the liquid to cool and wash the eyes with it as often as possible.

A more powerful lotion can be made by replacing the daisy flowers with white lily, valerian and the leaves of the rowan tree.

For sore eyes
This strange and ancient charge, or remedy, known as 'The Charge of the Artificer's Son', was inherited from the Vikings who raided and then settled on the east coast of Ireland in the ninth century. Take onions, dill, wormwood and garlic, mash them up and boil them in beer, then add the gall from a hog's liver and a drop of wine or doe's milk, strain well, pour into a brass amphora and apply to the eyes.

For freckles
Anoint the skin with the distilled water of walnuts.

For psoriasis and other skin complaints
Drink every day two cups of spring water which has been boiled and allowed to cool.

For burns
Make an ointment out of sheep's suet boiled with the rind of the elder tree. If this is used properly, it can heal the burn without leaving a scar.

For purging the system and lengthening life
Take a pound of raisins and soak them for two days in a covered basin full of warmed water from a mountain stream. Throughout the next day, eat nothing but the raisins and drink nothing but the water. This should

be done on one day in every month or for a whole
week once a year.

For reducing blood pressure
Eat the peel of a whole lemon every day until the
pressure is reduced.

For Jaundice
A salad made from various herbs and known as 'The
Green Ointment'. This is one of the most effective
cures ever devised for any malady, but the recipe is
known only to the wise women of the west and
unfortunately the author was unable to get any of
them to part with it.

For hangovers and indigestion
Four tablespoons of apple cider vinegar in a pint of
water. For hangovers, drink as many pints of this as
possible (apple cider vinegar on its own is also
excellent for sore throats and arthritis).

For melancholy
Whiskey punch – whiskey, sugar or honey, lemon and
hot water (spices can also be added).

THE CHARMS

♣

A charm to win the love of a woman:

Sit her down beside running water between a mill and a tree. Feed her butter on a new plate and whisper these words to yourself as she eats: 'O woman, loved by me, mayst thou give me thy heart, thy soul and thy body.'

A charm to win the love of a man:

Give him a glass of wine or spirits and whisper these words to yourself as he drinks: 'You for me and I for thee and for none else. Your face to mine and your head turned from all others.'

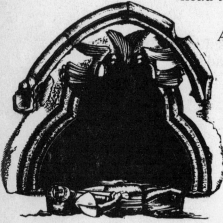

A charm to keep a man's love for ever:

Go to a graveyard by night. Find a corpse that has been exactly nine days dead and tear down a strip of the skin from head to foot. Then go to where the man

is sleeping, tie the strip round his arm or leg and leave it there until morning, removing it before he is awake. As long as the strip of skin is kept, secretly hidden from all eyes, the man will remain a faithful lover.

A charm to separate lovers:

Sprinkle a handful of clay from a newly made grave between them and whisper, 'May ye be as hateful to each other as sin to Christ or bread without blessing to God.'

A charm to bring on a vision of a future spouse:

Pass a piece of wedding cake three times through a wedding ring. Then sleep on it, and in your dream you will see the face of the person you will marry.

A charm for curing a burn:

Lay the right hand very softly over the burn and

breath gently on to it while repeating these words
very quietly three times:

> Old clod beneath the clay,
> Burn away, burn away.
> In the name of God, be thou healed. Amen.

This charm is much more effective if it is performed
by a widow who has the gift of second sight.
Furthermore it is usually possible to tell whether or
not the charm is going to work, because, if it is, the
patient tends to fall into a deep sleep.

A charm to reduce the pain of a burn:

This only works if it is done within a minute of the
burn taking place. Blow on to it three times, chanting
as follows each time:

> Two angels sat upon a stone,
> One was Fire, the other Frost,
> Praise Father, Son and Holy Ghost.

A charm to get rid of warts:

Stand on your doorstep at midnight under a full moon,
rub the warts seven times with a sliced raw potato
saying each time 'blemish be gone'. Then bury the
potato and say over it 'as this rots, so will my warts'.

Another charm to get rid of warts:

Rub the warts with mud that has been taken from the
shoes of men who have just carried the coffin in a

funeral; and keep this up for several minutes, concentrating steadily all the time on an image of the vanishing warts.

A charm to cure scrofula (the King's Evil):

This morbid condition was known throughout Europe in the Middle Ages as 'The King's Evil' because it was believed that it could be cured by the touch of a king. In Ireland, however, in addition, some families have a piece of paper or parchment which was once soaked in a king's blood. If this precious heirloom is rubbed over the patient in the name of the Trinity, the scrofula will depart.

A charm to cure Erysipelas (St Anthony's Fire):

This fever, which produces a deep red colouring of the skin, is known in Ireland as 'wild fire' and in England as 'St Anthony's fire'. It is said to be caused by the malice of fairies, and only the spilling of blood to appease them will cure it. The blood of a black cat is thought to be the most effective. As a result, there was a time when there were few black cats in Ireland that had an entire tail, little bits having been nipped off from time to time in order to effect a cure.

A charm to cure mumps in a child:

Tie a halter round the child's neck, lead the child to a brook and dip the child in the water three times in the name of the Trinity.

Another charm to cure mumps in a child:

Wrap the child in a blanket, take it to a pigsty and rub its head on the back of a pig. The disease will pass from the child to the beast.

A more powerful charm for curing mumps in an adult:

Gather nine black stones before sunrise. Put a rope round the patient's neck and lead him in silence to a holy well. Drop in three stones in the name of God, three more in the name of Christ and the last three in the name of Mary. Do this for three mornings and the mumps will be cured.

A charm to cure rickets in a child:

A blacksmith who is at least one of the fourth generation of his family to follow that calling must put the child in his apron and carry it three times round his anvil for seven days in succession repeating the Paternoster each time. (This will not work if the blacksmith receives any kind of payment.)

A charm for curing whooping cough:

Fast for a day. Then put a live trout into the mouth and keep it there for at least a minute. Then put it back in the river, and the disease will go with it. (If a trout cannot be found, a frog is sometimes equally effective.)

Two more, less obnoxious, charms to cure whooping cough:

(1) Fill a mug with water from a running stream, against the current. Then make the patient drink one large swallow and throw the rest away in the stream, with the current. Repeat this for at least three consecutive mornings before sunrise.

(2) Cut a lock of hair from the head of a man who never saw his father and tie it up in a piece of red cloth. This is to be worn constantly round the patient's neck until the coughing has completely stopped.

A charm to cure a toothache:

Go to a graveyard, kneel on a grave and say three paters and three Aves for the soul of the occupant. Then take a handful of grass from the grave, chew it well and spit out each bite, taking care not to swallow any. This will not only cure a toothache, it will also prevent the sufferer from ever having a toothache again.

Two more charms to cure a toothache:

(1) Drink water from a human skull.

(2) Take a pinch of clay from a priest's grave and hold it in your mouth for a while.

Charms for easing the pain of a toothache:

Rub the jaw outside the painful area with the tooth of a dead horse or the hand of a dead man – but remember, this will only help the pain. It will not cure it.

Charms to avoid toothache:

A woman should vow to God, the Virgin and the new moon that she will never comb her hair on a Friday; and a man should vow to the same three that he will never shave on a Sunday.

Charms to cure a cough:

(1) Eat a griddle cake left over from the breakfast of a husband and wife who had the same name before they married.

(2) Touch a piebald horse.

(3) Chop up nine hairs from a black cat's tail, mix them with water and drink the mixture.

(4) To cure a cough in a child, tie a red string round its throat and pass the child seven times under and over the body of an ass.

A charm to cure stomach disorders:

Simply tie a bunch of mint around the wrist.

A charm to cure dyspepsia:

Make the patient lie on his back. Take a small piece of candle, put it on top of a penny and put the penny on the patient's stomach. Light the candle, cover it with a well-dried tumbler and leave it until the candle has burnt out, intoning all the while, 'In the name of the Father and of the Son and of the Holy Ghost.' (This is very close to the traditional cure known as 'cupping' which is used all over the world, but in other cultures it is usually regarded as rather dangerous to place the cup over the stomach or the heart.)

A charm to reduce inflammation:

Take nine handfuls of mountain moss and dry them to a powder. Take nine pinches of the powder and nine pinches of ashes from the hearth, mix them in a bowl of whey and then drink a mouthful of the mixture every Tuesday and Thursday.

Two charms to cure a sty:

(1) Rub the whole eye with the tail of a black cat.

(2) Point a gooseberry-thorn at it nine times, chanting each time, 'Away, away, away.'

A charm to get rid of freckles:

To make a girl's skin clear and fair,
Rub well with the blood of a bull or a hare.

A charm to bring safety to a journey:

Pluck ten blades of yarrow, throw one away for the
fairies and put the other nine in your sock or stocking
under the heel of your right foot.

A charm to attract bees:

Gather foxglove, raspberry leaves, wild marjoram,
mint, camomile and valerian on May Day, mix them
with butter that has been made on May Day, add
honey and boil the whole mixture. Then rub the
mixture on the inside and outside of the vessel in
which you want the bees to make their hive and place
it in the middle of a tree.

THE SUPERSTITIONS

♣

It is very, very lucky to dream of horses.

It is unlucky to kill a robin redbreast.

It is unlucky to pass a churn and not offer a helping hand.

It is a bad omen if a hare crosses your path before sunrise.

If you meet a funeral, you can only avoid bad luck by turning and walking three steps beside it.

If you live in the country, do not stay up too late at night. The fairies may want to hold a meeting in your house and they will be merciless in their vengeance if you prevent them from doing so in secret. If you must stay up, make sure that there are animals with you, particularly cats, for the animals will know if the fairies are coming.

A long time ago there was an old woman who lived alone in one of the remotest parts of Donegal. One night when she had stayed up very late she thought she heard a scratching at her door and a voice calling, 'Judy, Judy, let me in.'

The first couple of times she ignored it, but when she heard it a third time she went to the door and found a black cat with a white nose and two white kittens waiting there in the rain. Thinking that this was the source of the scratching and that the voice had indeed been the wind, Judy let the cat and her kittens come in to warm themselves by her fire.

However, after a few minutes, the cat turned her head, looked up and said, 'Judy, why are you up so late?'

Judy stared at her in silent disbelief and astonishment.

The cat continued, 'The fairies are planning to meet here tonight. You must go to bed. If I had not delayed them and come on to warn you, they would have done you great harm. You must not do this again. Now, I have turned aside for you and I have far to go. Give us a bowl of milk and we will be on our way.'

Eggshells are a favourite hiding place for fairies. Always break the shell when you have eaten an egg, so that a fairy cannot take up residence in it.

Unbaptized children are easily kidnapped by fairies.
To prevent this, tie a little bag of salt into the
nightdress when the child is laid in its cradle.

The fairies are most powerful on a Friday. Never speak
ill of them on that day for they can hear everything.

Fairies are merry and mischievous. They like people
who are generous and considerate towards them.
That is why many people leave out food for them at
night and build up the fire for them before going to
bed; and that is why nobody in Ireland in the old days
would ever throw out water at night without
shouting, 'Take care of the water.' Fairies are very vain
and fastidious. If their bright clothes and little
feathered caps were to get a drenching, they could be
merciless in their retribution.

Fairies also hate anything that smacks of
meanness. Until recently in Connaught, when a child
spilled its milk, there would be no scolding; instead
the mother would say, 'That to the fairies. Leave it to
them and welcome.'

The devil, ghosts and evil spirits cannot cross running
water. If you fear that you are being pursued by night,
make for the nearest stream and cross it.

People who are born in the morning
will never have the power to see
ghosts or fairies. To do that,
you have to be born at night.

Walk three times round a fire on St John's Eve and you will be free from sickness for a year.

Anyone who dies as the clock strikes midnight between Christmas Eve and Christmas morning will go to Heaven immediately and escape purgatory.

No matter how terrible the storm, a boat will never, never sink if it is steered by a woman on her wedding day.

It is unlucky to stick a knife into the mast of a boat.

The spirit of the last person buried on any day in a graveyard becomes the servant of all the other souls in the graveyard until another corpse is buried there. On numerous occasions, all over Ireland, even in Dublin, this belief has led to unseemly races between funerals.

If a baby is born very small and weak, there is always a danger that it may in fact be a fairy changeling. A certain way of finding out whether it is or not is to put it on a shovel in front of the fire. If it is a fairy, after a while, as the shovel gets hot, it will fly up the chimney and vanish for ever.

The problem here is of course that a human child may be slowly

roasted to death in terrible agony before its innocence has been established.

It is unlucky to pick up an unbaptized child without making the sign of the cross over it first.

It is unlucky to start work on a Friday.

It is unlucky to move house or change job on a Saturday.

If you start to make a dress on a Saturday, the wearer will die within a year.

To bring good luck to travellers, throw a slipper after them just as they have begun their journey.

If you mend a torn dress while you are wearing it, people will spread malicious gossip about you.

Marry in autumn and die in spring.

It is unlucky to pay a debt on the first Monday of the year.

If a knot is tied in a red handkerchief on a wedding day, the marriage will be unhappy. The only way to break this spell is to find the handkerchief and burn it.

When a seventh son is born, an earth-worm must be put in the child's mouth and left there until it is dead. After that the child will have the power to cure all diseases.

Without the help of any spell, the seventh son of a seventh son will have the gift of second sight and the power to heal by the laying on of hands.

By using the power of a certain herb, the leprechauns know how to find all the crocks of gold that are hidden all over Ireland. But nobody has ever been able to persuade any of them to reveal the name of the herb.

All over the world, the asses kneel down in their stables on Christmas morning at the moment when Christ was born. If you can be in a stable at exactly this moment and if you can touch an ass on the back with a crucifix, your dearest wish will be granted.

A raven hovering over a house is a sure sign of impending evil, even death. To turn away this bad luck, chant as follows:

'May fire and water be in you,
Oh bird of evil;
And may the curse of God be on your head
For ever and ever and ever.'

It is unlucky to accept the gift of a lock of hair or a four-footed beast from a lover.

A family that breakfasts by candle-light on Christmas morning, will have good fortune throughout the coming year.

If on the night of Candlemas candles are lit in the name of each member of the family, the candles will burn out in the order in which the family members will die.

No corpse should be touched until at least two hours after its death, for the soul must be given time to settle quietly in its new resting place.

It is an unlucky omen if a chair falls as a person rises from it.

If a child's fingernails are cut before it is twelve months old, it will grow up with light fingers and become an insatiable thief.

It is unlucky to cross the path of horses that are pulling a plough.

There is nothing more unlucky than the breaking of a mirror.

Since the beginning of the seventeenth century it has been believed that Tuesdays are unlucky for the English royal family; Henry VIII, Edward VI, Queen Mary and Elizabeth I all died on a Tuesday.

A male child born in Trinity Week is fated to take a life. The only way to break this curse is to catch a little bird and hold it close to the child's hand until it dies.

If you find a four-leafed shamrock,
and if you always carry it with you
without telling anybody, you will
be lucky in all forms of gambling
and immune to witchcraft.

A purse made from the skin
of a weasel will never be
empty – but only if the user of
the purse found it, and did not
make it or receive it as a gift.

Always make the sign of the cross
when yawning, to prevent the evil spirit from rushing
down your throat and taking up residence within you.

It is unlucky to give away water before breakfast or to
give away milk from a farm during churning.

To discover whether or not a sick person will recover,
take nine smooth stones from running water, fling
them over the right shoulder and then lay them in a
turf fire for the night. Strike the stones together in the
morning, and if they make a clear sound like a bell,
the disease will end in death.

If a married woman walks on a grave, her next child
will have a club-foot. If she steps on the grave by
accident, she can avoid this fate by kneeling down at
once, saying the Lord's prayer and making the sign of
the cross three times on the sole of her shoe.

The banshees, the fairy spirits of doom, only
appear to aristocrats. They are themselves
the spirits of beautiful young ladies from
the finest families who cannot enter
Heaven until another equally well-
bred and beautiful young lady has
died to take their place.

The appearance of a banshee is not in itself an ill
omen, but once she starts to weep and howl, a death
in a noble family is certain.

In the seat of the O'Neils, Shane's Castle, a special
chamber has been set aside for a banshee, which is

sometimes seen in a mist-like cloak and sometimes in a scarlet mantle with a golden brooch.

It is unlucky to meet a cat, a dog or a woman first thing after leaving your house in the morning.

To give a magistrate or a judge insight and a true sense of justice, women should throw wheat and salt over him when he makes his way to take up his office for the first time.

If you meet a redheaded woman in the morning when you are setting out on a journey, turn back: her presence is a certain sign of evil.

If a hen crows, it is bewitched by fairies and must be killed at once.

An itching palm is a sign that you will be getting money.

An itching elbow is a sign that you will be changing beds.

An itching ear is a sign that someone is speaking ill of you.

A white-thorn walking-stick is unlucky in Ireland, but a hazel stick is very lucky and has the power to hold off the devil.

THE BLESSINGS AND
THE CURSES
♣

BLESSINGS

May you be through the gates of Heaven before the
devil knows you're dead.

God bless all here, except the cat.

May the shadow of the doctor never cross your arm.

May you never live to see your wife a widow.

Strength to your elbow.

God bless your work.

May many tears fall on your grave.

Good health and long life to you,
The woman of your choice to you,
Land without rent to you,
And may you die in Ireland.

CURSES

May you have a lawsuit in
which you know you are in
the right.

May you never have a day's luck.

May you die without a priest.

May you never hear another cuckoo.

'May you be hanged' is a curse for which there are
several slyly euphemistic Irish versions. One, alluding
to the victim's kicking heels, is 'May you die dancing'.
Another, inspired by the inevitable crowd of
spectators and the coffin waiting below the scaffold,
is 'May you live to see your own funeral.'

The Irish also have a poignant version of 'may you die
drowning' – 'The death of the kittens to you.'

An all-purpose curse, which can be used to bring
anything from death and destruction to an attack of
piles or (in County Wexford) rheumatism, refers to a
brief but terrible moment in Irish history – it is
simply 'the curse of Cromwell on you'.

Another historical curse comes from the fall of the
great Irish Nationalist leader Charles Stewart Parnell,
after he had been cited as co-respondent in a divorce.
When a family has no sons, it is said to be the victim
of Parnell's curse.

The curse of the Dead Hand can be used to inflict any
suffering on a victim. All that is necessary is to hold a
human hand that has been preserved by drying or
smoking and imagine the intended evil. But a dead

hand is useless if it has been inherited. The curse will only be effective if the user of the hand is also the person who went to a graveyard and cut the hand from a recently buried corpse at midnight.

A glance from a person who has 'The Evil Eye' can cause animals, and sometimes people, to waste away and die. People possessed of this power can usually be identified by a low brow and sunken eyes. If someone is suspected of having the power, it can sometimes be neutralized before it is used by staring back at them and saying, 'The curse be upon thine own eye.'

The power of the evil eye is at its strongest on Mayday Eve, when it is wise to protect cattle by sprinkling oatmeal on their backs, bleeding them and tasting their blood. If at any time you suspect that your cattle have been glanced at by someone with the evil eye, the only way to break the curse is to drive them to a holy well and pray all the time while they are drinking. If, however, you happen to glance at a graveyard while on your way to the well, this antidote will not work.

A frighteningly simple curse which will cause a person to pine away and die involves no more than burying a lighted candle in their name in a churchyard. This curse is so powerful that the only way of nullifying it is by finding the candle and eating it – and even then the antidote does not always work. A man in Letterkenny who was cursed by a jilted lover managed to find the candle after nine days of frantic searching, but, although he ate it, he still died within the month. The power of the curse and the broken heart behind it was too much.

It should be noted, however, that this curse will only work if the burying of the candle is performed in strict accordance with a weird and ancient ceremony. The order of this ceremony was originally included in this text, but wise women warned that it was extremely dangerous to impart such information to a wide readership and that so doing might put the

author and publishers in danger of being cursed
themselves. In consequence the order of the ceremony
has been withdrawn.

A FEW OF THE SONGS

MOLLY MALONE

In Dublin's fair city, where the girls are so pretty,
I first set my eyes on sweet Molly Malone,
She wheeled a wheel-barrow through streets broad
    and narrow,
Crying, 'Cockles and Mussels, a-live, a-live oh.'

Chorus: A-live, A-live Oh, A-live A-live Oh,
             Crying: Cockles and Mussels, A-live, A-live Oh!

She was a fishmonger, but sure, 'twas no wonder,
For so were her father and mother before;
And they both wheeled their barrow, through streets
    broad and narrow,
Crying, 'Cockles and Mussels, a-live, a-live oh.'

She died of a fever, and no one could save her,
And that was the end of sweet Molly Malone,
But her ghost wheels her barrow, through streets
    broad and narrow,
Crying, 'Cockles and Mussels, a-live, a-live oh.'

THE ROSE OF TRALEE

The pale moon was rising above the green mountains,
The sun was declining beneath the blue sea,
When I stray'd with my love to the pure crystal
   fountain,
That stands in the beautiful vale of Tralee.
She was lovely and fair as the rose of the summer,
Yet 'twas not her beauty alone that won me,
Oh no, 'twas the truth in her eye ever dawning,
That made me love Mary, the Rose of Tralee.

The cool shades of evening their mantles were
   spreading,
And Mary, all smiles, sat list'ning to me,
The moon thro' the valley, her pale rays were
   shedding
When I won the heart of the Rose of Tralee.
Yet 'twas not her beauty alone that won me,
Oh no, 'twas truth in her eye ever dawning,
That made me love Mary, the Rose of Tralee.

THE SPANISH LADY

As I went down to Dublin city, at the hour of twelve at
   night,
Who should I see but a Spanish lady, washing her feet
   by candle light,
First she washed them, then she dried them, over a
   fire of amber coal,
In all my life I ne'er did see a maid so sweet about
   the sole,

Chorus: Whack fol the too-ra, loo-ra, lad-dy,
         Whack fol the too-ra loo-ra-lay.

As I came back through Dublin city
At the hour of half past eight,
Who should I spy but the Spanish Lady
Brushing her hair in the broad daylight;
First she tossed it, then she brushed it.
On her lap was a silver comb.
In all my life I ne'er did see
A maid so fair since I did roam.

Chorus

As I went back through Dublin city
As the sun began to set,
Who should I spy but the Spanish Lady
Catching a moth in a golden net;
When she saw me then she fled me
Lifting her petticoat over her knee

In all my life I ne'er did see
A maid so shy as the Spanish Lady.

Chorus

I've wandered north and I've wandered south
Through Stonybatter and Patrick's Close
Up and around the Gloster Diamond
And back by Napper Tandy's house:
Old age has laid her hand on me
Cold as a fire of ashy coals.
In all my life I ne'er did see
A maid so sweet as the Spanish Lady.

Chorus

THE WILD ROVER

I've been a wild rover for many's the year,
And I've spent all me money on whiskey and beer,
And now I'm returning with gold in great store,
And I never will play the wild rover no more,

Chorus: And it's No, Nay, Never, No Nay Never No more,
            Will I play the wild rover, No, Never No more.

I went to an alehouse I used to frequent
And I told the landlady my money was spent
I asked her for credit she answered me 'Nay,
Such custom as yours could I have every day.'

Chorus

I brought up from my pockets ten sovereigns bright,
And the landlady's eyes opened wide with delight.
She said 'I have whiskeys and wines of the best,
And the words that I told you were only in jest.'

Chorus

I'll go home to my parents, confess what I've done,
And I'll ask them to pardon their prodigal son.
And when they've caressed me as oft times before,
I never will play the wild rover no more.

Chorus

151

WHISKEY IN THE JAR

As I was going over, the Kilmagenny mountain,
I met with Captain Farrell and his money he was
   counting,
I first produced me pistol, and then I drew my sabre,
Saying 'Stand and deliver for I am a bold deceiver.'

Chorus: With me ring dum a doodle um dah,
       whack fol the daddy o,
       whack fol the daddy o,
       there's whiskey in the jar.

He counted out his money and it made a pretty penny,
I put it in my pocket and I gave it to my Jenny,
She sighed and she swore that she never would betray me,
But the devil take the women for they never can be easy.

I went into my chamber all for to take a slumber,
I dreamt of gold and jewels and for sure it was no
   wonder,
But Jenny drew my charges and she filled them up
   with water
And she went for Captain Farrell to be ready for the
   slaughter.

And 'twas early in the morning before I rose to travel,
Up comes a band of footmen and likewise Captain
   Farrell;
I then produced my pistol, for she stole my sabre,
But I couldn't shoot the water, so a prisoner I was taken.

And if anyone can aid me, it's my brother in the army,
If I could learn his station in Cork or in Killarney,
And if he'd come and join me, we'd go roving in
    Kilkenny.
I'll engage he'd treat me fairer than my darling
    sporting Jenny.

THE MINSTREL BOY

The minstrel boy to the war is gone,
in the ranks of death you'll find him
His father's sword he has girded on
and his wild harp slung behind him.

'Land of song,' said the warrior bard,
'Though all the world betray thee,
One sword at least thy right shall guard,
One faithful harp shall praise thee.'

The minstrel fell – but the foeman's chain
Could not bring his proud soul under.
The harp he lov'd ne'er spoke again
For he tore its chords asunder.

And said, 'No chains shall sully thee,
Thou soul of love and bravery!
Thy songs were made for the pure and free,
They shall never sound in slavery.'

Thomas Moore

KITTY OF COLERAINE

As beautiful Kitty one morning was tripping
With a pitcher of milk from the fair at Coleraine,
When she saw me she stumbled, the pitcher down
    tumbled,
And all the sweet butter-milk watered the plain.
'Oh what shall I do now? 'twas lookin' at you now;
Sure, sure, such a pitcher I'll ne'er meet again;
'Twas the pride of my dairy! O Barney MacCleary,
You're sent as a plague to the girls of Coleraine!'

I sat down beside her and gently did chide her
That such a misfortune should give her such pain;
A kiss then I gave her, and ere I did leave her,
She vowed for such pleasure she'd break it again.
'Twas hay-making season – I can't tell the reason –
Misfortunes will never come single, 'tis plain;
For very soon after poor Kitty's disaster
The devil a pitcher was whole in Coleraine.

'JOHNNY I HARDLY KNEW YE'

While going the road to sweet Athy,
   Hurroo! Hurroo!
While going the road to sweet Athy,
   Hurroo! Hurroo!
While going the road to sweet Athy,
A stick in my hand, and a drop in my eye,
A doleful damsel I heard cry:
'Och Johnny, I hardly knew ye!'

Chorus: With their drums and guns and guns and
        drums,
      The enemy nearly slew ye,
      Och, John me dear, you look so queer,
      Johnny I hardly knew ye!

Where are your eyes that looked so mild?
   Hurroo! Hurroo!
Where are your eyes that looked so mild?
   Hurroo! Hurroo!
Where are your eyes that looked so mild?
Where my poor heart you first beguiled?
Arah, why did you run from me and the child?
Och, Johnny, I hardly knew ye!

Chorus

Where are the legs with which you run?
   Hurroo! Hurroo!
Where are the legs with which you run?

Hurroo! Hurroo!
Where are the legs with which you run?
When first you went to carry your gun?
Indeed your dancing days are done!
Och, Johnny, I hardly knew ye!

Chorus

It grieved my heart to see you sail,
  Hurroo! Hurroo!
It grieved my heart to see you sail,
  Hurroo! Hurroo!
It grieved my heart to see you sail,
Though from my heart you took leg-bail;
Like a cod you're doubled up head and tail,
Och, Johnny, I hardly knew ye!

Chorus

You haven't an arm and you haven't a leg,
  Hurroo! Hurroo!
You haven't an arm and you haven't a leg,
  Hurroo! Hurroo!
You haven't an arm and you haven't a leg,
You're an eyeless, noseless, chickenless egg,
You'll have to be put with a bowl to beg:
Och, Johnny I hardly knew ye!

Chorus

I'm happy for to see you home,
   Hurroo! Hurroo!
I'm happy for to see you home,
   Hurroo! Hurroo!
I'm happy for to see you home,
All from the Island of Sulloon;
So low in flesh, so high in bone,
Och, Johnny I hardly knew ye!

Chorus

But sad it is to see you so,
   Hurroo! Hurroo!
But sad it is to see you so,
   Hurroo! Hurroo!
But sad it is to see you so,
And to think of you now as an object of woe,
But your Peggy will keep you as her beau;
Och, Johnny, I hardly knew ye!

Chorus

THE GIRL I LEFT BEHIND ME

Come all ye handsome comely maids
That live near Carlow dwelling.
Beware of young men's flatt'ring tongue
When love to you they're telling.
Beware of the kind words they say,
Be wise and do not mind them,
For if they were talking till they die
They'd leave you all behind them.

In Carlow town I lived I own
All free from debt and danger.
Till Colonel Reilly listed me
To join the Wicklow Rangers.
They dressed me up in scarlet red
And they used me very kindly
But still I thought my heart would break
For the girl I left behind me.

I was scarcely fourteen years of age
When I was broken-hearted,
For I'm in love these two long years
Since from my love I parted.
These maidens wonder how I moan
And bid me not to mind him
That he might have more grief than joy
For leaving me behind him.

I KNOW WHERE I'M GOIN'

I know where I'm goin',
And I know who's goin' with me,
I know who I love
But the dear knows who I'll marry!

I have stockings of silk,
Shoes of fine green leather,
Combs to buckle my hair,
And a ring for every finger.

Some say he's black,
But I say he's bonny,
The fairest of them all
My handsome, winsome Johnny.

Feather beds are soft,
And painted rooms are bonny,
But I would leave them all
To go with my love Johnny.

THE OCTOBER WINDS

The October winds lament around
The castle of Dromore,
Yet peace is in her lofty halls –
My loving treasure-store.
Though Autumn leaves may droop and die,
A bud of spring are you.
Sing hushabye lul, lul, lo, lo, lan,
Sing hushabye lul, lul, loo.

Bring no ill-will to hinder us,
My helpless babe and me,
Dread spirit of the Black Water,
Clan Eoin's wild banshee;
And holy Mary pitying us
In Heaven for grace shall sue.
Sing hushabye lul, lul, lo, lo, lan,
Sing hushabye lul, lul, loo.

Take time to thrive, my rose of hope,
In the garden of Dromore;
Take heed young eaglet till your wings
Are feathered fit to soar;
A little while and then the world
Is full of work to do.
Sing hushabye lul, lul, lo, lo, lan,
Sing hushabye lul, lul, loo.

A STAR OF THE COUNTY DOWN

Near Banbridge town in the County Down one
   morning last July
Down a boreen green came a sweet cailin and she
   smiled as she passed me by.
She looked so neat from her two bare feet to the
   crown of her nut brown hair,
Such a winsome elf I was ashamed of myself for to
   see I was really there.

Chorus: From Bantry Bay up to Derry quay and from
            Galway to Dublin town,
          No maid I've seen like the brown cailin that I
            met in the County Down.

As she onward sped sure I scratch'd my head and I
   looked with a feeling rare,
And I says, says I, to a passerby, 'Who's the maid with
   the nut brown hair?'
He smiled at me and he says to me, 'That's the gem of
   Ireland's crown,
Young Rosie McCann from the banks of the Bann,
   she's the star of the County Down.'

Chorus

At the harvest fair she'll be surely there, so I'll dress in
   my Sunday clothes;
With my shoes shone bright and my hat cocked right
   for a smile from the nut-brown Rose.

No pipe I'll smoke, no horse I'll yoke till my plough is
   a rust coloured brown,
Till a-smiling bright by my own fireside is the star
   from the County Down.

Chorus

THE OULD ORANGE FLUTE

In the County Tyrone, in the town of Dungannon,
Where many a ruction myself had a han' in,
Bob Williamson lived, a weaver by trade,
And as all of us thought him a stout Orange blade.
On the twelfth of July, as it yearly did come,
Bob played on the flute to the sound of the drum;
And although you may talk of the harp or the lute,
There was nothing could sound like Bob's ould
Orange flute.

But this treacherous scoundrel he took us all in,
For he married a Paypish called Bridget M'Ginn;
And turned Paypish himself, and forsook the ould cause
That gave us our freedom, religion and laws.
Now, the boys in the townland made some noise upon it,
And Bob had to fly to the province of Connacht.
He fled with his wife and his fixings to boot,
And along with the rest went the ould Orange flute.

At chapel on Sundays to atone for past deeds,
He said Pater and Ave and counted his beads,
Till, after some time, at the priest's own desire,
He went with his ould flute to play in the choir.
He went with his ould flute to play in the Mass,
And the instrument shivered and sighed, 'Oh, alas!'
And blow as he would, though it made a great noise,
The flute would play only the 'Protestant Boys'.
Bob jumped, humphed and started and got in a splutter,
And threw his ould flute in the blest Holy Water;

He thought that this charm would bring some other
   soun'
And he blew it but then it played 'Croppies Lie Down!'
And all he could whistle, and finger, and blow,
To play Paypish music the flute would not go;
'Kick the Pope', 'The Boyne Water', it always would
   sound,
But one Paypish squeak in it could not be found.

At a council of priests that was held the next day
They prepared to administer auto-da-fay;
As they couldn't knock heresy out of its head,
They bought Bob another to play in its stead.
So the ould flute was doomed, and its fate was pathetic,
It was fastened and burned at the stake as heretic.
And while the flames roared they all heard a strange
   noise,
'Twas the ould flute still playin' the 'Protestant Boys'!

THE WEARING OF THE GREEN

Oh Paddy dear, and did you hear the news that's
    going round?
The shamrock is forbid by law to grow on Irish ground:
Saint Patrick's day no more we'll keep, his colour
    can't be seen,
For there's a cruel law agin the wearing of the Green.
I met with Napper Tandy and he took me by the hand,
And said he, How's poor old Ireland, and how does
    she stand?
She's the most distressful country that ever yet was seen;
They're hanging men and women for the wearing of
    the Green.

Then since the colour we must wear is England's
    cruel Red,
'Twill serve us to remind us of the blood that has been
    shed;
You may take the shamrock from your hat and cast it
    on the sod,
But never fear, 'twill take root there, though underfoot
    'tis trod.
When laws can stop the blades of grass from growing
    as they grow,
And when the leaves in summer time their verdure
    dare not show,
Then I will change the colour that I wear in my
    caubeen;
But till that day, please God, I'll stick to wearing of
    the Green.

SHLATHERY'S MOUNTED FUT

You've heard o' Julius Caesar, an' the great Napoleon, too,
An' how the Cork Militia beat the Turks at Waterloo;
But there's a page of glory that, as yet, remains uncut,
An' that's the Martial story o' the Shlathery's Mounted
   Fut.
This gallant corps was organized by Shlathery's eldest son.
A noble-minded poacher, wid a double-breasted gun;
And many a head was broken, aye, an' many an eye
   was shut,
Whin practisin' manoeuvres in the Shlathery's
   Mounted Fut.

Chorus: An' down from the mountains came the
               squadrons an' platoons,
            An' whin we marched behind the dhrum to
               patriotic tunes,
            We felt that fame would gild the name o'
               Shlathery's Light Dhragoons.

Well, first we reconnoithered round o' O'Sullivan's
   Shebeen –
It used to be 'The Shop House', but we call it, 'The
   Canteen';
But there we saw a notice which the bravest heart
   unnerved –
'All liquor must be settled for before the dhrink is
   served.'
So on we marched, but soon again each warrior's
   heart grew pale,

For risin' high in front o' us we saw the County Jail;
An' whin the army faced about, 'twas just in time to find
A couple o' big policemin had surrounded us behind.

Chorus: Still down from the mountains came the
squadrons and platoons,
Four-an'-twinty fightin' min, an' a couple o'
sthout gossoons;
Says Shlathery, 'We must circumvent these
bludgeonin' bosthoons,
Or else it sames they'll take the names o'
Shlathery's Light Dhragoons.

'We'll cross the ditch,' our leader cried, 'an' take the
foe in flank,'
But yells of consthernation here arose from every rank,
For posted high upon a tree we very plainly saw,
'Thresspassers prosecuted, in accordance wid' the law.'
'We're foiled!' exclaimed bowld Shlathery, 'here ends
our grand campaign,
'Tis merely throwin' life away to face that mearin'
dhrain,
I'm not as bold as lions, but I'm braver nor a hin,
An' he that fights and runs away will live to fight agin.'

Chorus: And back to the mountains went the
squadrons and platoons,
Four-an'-twinty fightin' min, an' a couple o'
sthout gossoons;
The band was playing cautiously their
patriotic tunes;

> To sing the fame, if rather lame o' Shlathery's
> Light Dhragoons.

They reached the mountains safely, tho' all stiff and
   sore wi' cramp.
Each took a whet of whiskey neat to dissipate the damp;
And when they loaded all their pipes bold Shlathery
   ups and said,
'Today's a mortal fight will be remembered by the dead.
I niver shall forget,' said he, 'while this brave heart
   shall beat,
The eager way you follow'd me when I headed the
   retreat.
You preferred the soldier's maxim when disistin' from
   the strife,
"Best be a coward for five minutes than a dead man
   all your life."'

Chorus: And there in the mountains lay in squadrons
            and platoons
         Four-an'-twinty fightin' min an' a couple o'
            sthout gossoons;
         They niver more will march again to patriotic
            tunes,
         But all the same they sing the fame of
            Shlathery's Light Dhragoons.

THE MOUNTAINS OF MOURNE

Oh, Mary this London's a wonderful sight
With the people here working by day and by night,
They don't sow potatoes nor barley nor wheat,
But there's gangs of them digging for gold in the street,
At least when I asked them that's what I was told,
So I just took a hand at this digging for gold,
But for all that I found there I might as well be,
Where the mountains of Mourne sweep down to the sea.

I believe that when writing a wish you expressed
As to how the fine ladies of London were dressed.
Well if you believe me, when asked to a ball
They don't wear a top to their dresses at all,
Oh, I've seen them myself, and you could not in truth
Say if they were bound for a ball or a bath –
Don't be starting them fashions now Mary Macree,
Where the mountains of Mourne sweep down to the sea.

I've seen England's king from the top of a bus –
I never knew him, though he means to know us;
And though by the Saxon we once were oppressed,
Still, I cheered – God forgive me – I cheered with
   the rest.
And now that he's visited Erin's green shore,
We'll be much better friends than we've been
   heretofore.
When we've got all we want we're as quiet as can be,
Where the mountains of Mourne sweep down to the sea.

You remember young Peter O'Loughlin of course –
Well, now he is here at the head of the Force.
I met him today, I was crossing the Strand,
And he stopped the whole street with one wave of
    his hand;
And there we stood talking of days that are gone,
While the whole population of London looked on;
But for all these great powers he's wishful, like me,
To be back where dark Mourne sweeps down to the sea.

There's beautiful girls here – oh, never you mind
With beautiful shapes Nature never designed,
And lovely complexions, all roses and cream
But O'Loughlin remarked with regard to the same;
That if at those roses you venture to sip,
The colours might all come away on your lip;
So I'll wait for the wild rose that's waiting for me,
Where the mountains of Mourne sweep down to the sea.

Percy French

THE SHAN VAN VOCHT

'Oh! the French are on the say,'
Says the Shan Van Vocht;
'Oh! the French are on the say,'
Says the Shan Van Vocht.
'Oh! the French are in the bay –
They'll be here at break of day,
And the orange will decay,'
Says the Shan Van Vocht;
'And the orange will decay,'
Says the Shan Van Vocht.

'And where will they have their camp?'
Says the Shan Van Vocht;
'And where will they have their camp?'
Says the Shan Van Vocht.
'On the Curragh of Kildare,
And the boys will all be there,
With their pikes in good repair,'
Says the Shan Van Vocht;
'With their pikes in good repair,'
Says the Shan Van Vocht.

'And what colour will be seen?'
Says the Shan Van Vocht;
'And what colour will be seen?'
Says the Shan Van Vocht.
'What colour should be seen

Where our fathers' homes have been
But our own immortal green,'
Says the Shan Van Vocht;
'But our own immortal green,'
Says the Shan Van Vocht.

'Will old Ireland then be free?'
Says the Shan Van Vocht;
'Will old Ireland then be free?'
Says the Shan Van Vocht.
'Old Ireland shall be free,
From the centre to the sea –
Then hurrah for liberty!'
Says the Shan Van Vocht;
'Then hurrah for liberty!'
Says the Shan Van Vocht.

SHE MOVED THROUGH THE FAIR

My young love said to me, 'My mother won't mind
And my father won't slight you for your lack of kind.'
And she stepp'd away from me and this she did say,
'It will not be long love, till our wedding day.'

She stepp'd away from me and went thro' the fair,
And fondly I watch'd her move here and move there,
And then she went homeward with one star awake,
As the swan in the evening moves over the lake.

Last night she came to me, she came softly in,
So softly she came that her feet made no din.
And she laid her hand on me and this she did say,
'It will not be long, love, till our wedding day.'

CARRICKFERGUS

I wish I was in Carrickfergus,
Only for nights in Balligran,
I would swim over the deepest ocean,
The deepest ocean my love to find,
But the sea is wide and I cannot swim over,
And neither have I the wings to fly,
If I could find me a handsome boatman
To ferry me over to my love and die.

My childhood days bring back sad reflections
Of happy times I spent so long ago,
My boyhood friends and my own relations
Have passed on now like melting snow.
But I'll spend my days in endless roaming,
Soft is the grass, my bed is free.
Ah! to be back now in Carrickfergus,
On that long road down to the sea.

And in Kilkenny, it is reported,
They've marble stones there as black as ink.
With gold and silver I would support her,
But I'll sing no more now 'till I get a drink.
I'm drunk today, but I'm seldom sober,
A handsome rover from town to town.
Ah, but I'm sick now, my days are numbered,
Come all ye young men and lay me down.

DANNY BOY

Oh, Danny boy, the pipes, the pipes are calling,
From glen to glen and down the mountainside,
The summer's gone and all the roses falling,
'Tis you, 'tis you must go and I must bide,
But come ye back when summer's in the meadow,
Or when the valley's hushed and white with snow.
'Tis I'll be there in sunshine or in shadow,
Oh Danny boy, Oh Danny boy I love you so.

And when you come and all the flowers are dying,
If I am dead – and dead I well may be,
Ye'll come and find a place where I am lying,
And kneel and say an Ave there for me;
And I shall hear though soft your tread above me,
And all my grave shall warmer, sweeter be,
For you will bend and tell me that you love me,
And I shall live in peace until you come to me.

(These verses, written in the first quarter of this century by Fred Weatherly, are the words most often sung to one of the most ancient and haunting Irish melodies, 'The Derry Air'.)

I'LL TELL MY MA

I'll tell my ma when I go home,
The boys won't leave the girls alone,
They pull my hair, they stole my comb.
But that's all right 'till I go home.
She is handsome, she is pretty,
She is the belle of Belfast City,
She is courtin' one, two, three,
Please won't you tell me who is she?

Albert Mooney says he loves her,
All the boys are fighting for her,
They rap at the door, and they ring the bell,
Saying O my true love are you well?
Out she comes as white as snow,
Rings on her fingers, bells on her toes,
Old Johnny Murray says she'll die,
If she doesn't get the fellow with the roving eye.

I KNOW MY LOVE

I know my love by his way of walking,
And I know my love by his way of talking,
And I know my love dressed in his jersey blue,
And if my love leaves me, what will I do?

Chorus: And still she cried, 'I love him best,
    And a tiring mind can know no rest,'
    And still she cried, 'Bonny boys are few.
    And if my love leaves me, what will I do?'

There is a dance house down in Mata dyke,
And there my true love goes every night,
And takes a strange one upon his knee,
And don't you think now that vexes me?

If my love knew I could wash and wring,
If my love knew I could weave and spin,
I'd make a coat all of the finest kind,
But the want of money sure leaves me behind.

Chorus